THE BEST
YEARS OF THE
BEATLES

THE BEST YEARS OF THE BEATLES

PETE BEST

WITH

BILL HARRY

HEADLINE

First published in 1996
by HEADLINE BOOK PUBLISHING LTD

First published in softback in 1997
by HEADLINE BOOK PUBLISHING LTD

10 9 8 7 6 5 4 3 2 1

ISBN 0 7472 7762 1

Typeset by Letterpart Limited,
Reigate, Surrey

Repro by Fotographics

Designed by Peter Ward

Printed and bound in Great Britain by
Butler & Tanner Ltd, Frome and London

HEADLINE BOOK PUBLISHING
A division of Hodder Headline PLC
338 Euston Road
London NW1 3BH

To Beatles fans throughout the world

ALSO BY BILL HARRY

Arrows
Mersey Beat: The Beginning of the Beatles
Heroes of the Spaceways
The Beatles Who's Who
The Book of Lennon
The Book of Beatles Lists
Ask Me Why: The Beatles Quizbook
The Beatles
Beatlemania: The Beatles on Film
Beatles for Sale
Paperback Writers
The McCartney File
Sgt Pepper's Lonely Hearts Club Band
The Ultimate Beatles Encyclopedia
The Encyclopedia of Beatles People

ACKNOWLEDGEMENTS

I would like to thank Pete's brother, Roag Best, for all his help in bringing this book to fruition. He has been invaluable in providing information about Pete's early years and as a point of contact during Pete's absence on tour with his new band. My thanks also go to all at Headline for their encouragement while I was writing the book.

BILL HARRY

CONTENTS

THE BEST YEARS
OF THE BEATLES

▶ INTRODUCTION

BY BILL HARRY

Pete Best took early retirement in 1993 from a job as a civil servant he had been patiently attending for a quarter of a century. During those years he might have become one of the most famous men in the century, a household name, a multi-millionaire with an extravagant lifestyle and homes in various countries in the world.

Instead, he led a quiet domestic life in a suburban area of Liverpool, settling down with his wife Kathy and rearing their two daughters Beba and Bonita.

Pete was a Beatle, a member of the most celebrated group in history – and his dreams were shattered when he was unceremoniously sacked when they were on the brink of fame. There was no proper explanation, no compensation, nor did he meet again the three who had been his close comrades for two dynamic years during which they ate, slept, drank, caroused together and forged a sound which conquered the world.

The following years in which the Beatles' careers grew spectacularly must have been painful for someone who had played his part and deserved to be up there with them, but in the end it was Peter's strong character that prevailed.

Pete Best has always been acknowledged as a trustworthy and honourable person, a good and reliable friend to those who know him, and in all those years he has never had a bad word to say against his former colleagues.

In *The Best Years of the Beatles*, Pete describes in his own words those exciting times. I have tried not to intrude on his story, considering it best to leave him to tell his tale almost verbatim, but adding my personal commentary to each chapter. Once again, there is an absence of bitterness. He looks back at those times with affection, with no attempt to poison the memories with recriminations.

I am glad to say that the story has a happy ending. When Pete retired in 1993, he

Left: The famous Astrid Kirchherr shot of the five Beatles at Der Dom (The Dome) in Hamburg, which appeared on the cover of issue No. 2 of *Mersey Beat*. This was the first significant image of the Beatles to be published, and the only shot by Astrid which included the full group line-up at the time. (Astrid Kirchherr/Redferns)

Bill and Virginia Harry (née Sowry) at the Jacaranda club in June 1960, the month that Pete Best made his debut there as a member of the Beatles. Behind them is a mural painted by Stuart Sutcliffe and Rod Murray. The Beatles first appeared there on 30 May 1960.

teamed up with one of his younger brothers, Roag, in Splash Promotions, formed his own group, the Pete Best Band, and suddenly found the fame that had eluded him for thirty years.

He toured forty cities in Japan, fêted, celebrated, appreciated. Canadian tours followed, then a world tour. Pete was now appearing on major television shows such as 'The Oprah Winfrey Show', in television commercials – and was even the subject of a stage play. The icing on the cake came when a number of tracks he recorded with the Beatles were featured on the 'Anthology I' CD release.

His new-found fame won't end there. A television documentary is on its way, Hollywood is negotiating for a screen biopic, record companies are seeking his signature on contracts, new CDs are being recorded, and he's even been booked to star on a luxury Caribbean cruise. A Beatle has come in out of the cold.

The birthplace of the Beatles was a cellar club in Liverpool called the Casbah, run by the city's premier female promoter, Mona Best. But for the opening of the Casbah in August 1959, the Beatles might never have existed.

John Lennon's group the Quarry Men had disbanded several months previously. Although Paul McCartney and John Lennon occasionally met to pen songs together, they no longer performed as a group. George Harrison was a member of an outfit called the Les Stewart Quartet.

John, Paul and George re-formed as the Quarry Men for their first-ever residency and from the cellars of the Casbah, their road to riches began. In August 1960, when the opportunity arose for them to perform in Hamburg, they asked Mona Best's son, Pete Best, to be their drummer and finally settled on the name of the Beatles.

Hamburg proved to be their 'baptism of fire', and the group were transformed into a powerhouse of talent, playing several hours a night in the rough clubs of the St Pauli red light district. It was here that Pete Best was to develop 'the atom beat', a dramatic drum style which was to be copied by many musicians back home in Liverpool.

With their black leather outfits, electrifying volume and powerful stage show developed during the months in Hamburg, they shook the local music scene on Merseyside, beginning with their dynamic performance at the Casbah on 17 December 1960.

In his first major article in the *Mersey Beat* newspaper, local disc jockey Bob Wooler only mentioned one Beatle by name: 'the mean, moody and magnificent Pete Best'. Girls used to sleep overnight in his garden just to be near him and some

WELL NOW —DIG THIS!

BY BOB WOOLER

Why do you think The Beatles are so popular? Many people many times have asked me this question since that fantastic night (Tuesday, 27th December 1960) at Litherland Town Hall, when the impact of the act was first felt on this side of the River. I consider myself privileged to have been associated with the launching of the group on that exciting occasion, and grateful for the opportunities of presenting them to fever-pitch audiences at practically all of the group's subsequent appearances prior to their last Hamburg trip.

Perhaps my close association with the group's activities, both earlier this year and since their recent re-appearance on the Merseyside scene, persuades people to think that I can produce a blueprint of The Beatles Success Story. It figures, I suppose, and if, in attempting to explain the popularity of their act, the following analysis is at variance with other peoples views, well that's just one of those things. The question is nevertheless thought-provoking.

Well, then how to answer it? First some obvious observations. The Beatles are the biggest thing to have hit the Liverpool rock 'n' roll set-up in years. They were, and still are, the hottest local property any Rock promoter is likely to encounter. To many of these gentlemen's ears, Beatle-brand noises are cacophonous on stage, but who can ignore the fact that the same sounds translate into the sweet-est music this side of heaven at the box-office!

I think The Beatles are No. 1 because they resurrected original style rock 'n' roll music, the origins of which are to be found in American negro singers. They hit the scene when it had been emasculated by figures like Cliff Richard and sounds like those electronic wonders, The Shadows and their many imitators. Gone was the drive that inflamed the emotions. This was studio set jungle music purveyed skilfully in a chartwise direction by arrangement with the A & R men.

The Beatles, therefore, exploded on a jaded scene. And to those people on the verge of quitting teendom—those who had experienced during their most impressionable years the impact of rhythm 'n' blues music (raw rock 'n' roll)—this was an experience, a process of regaining and reliving a style of sounds and associated feelings identifiable with their era.

Here again, in The Beatles, was the stuff that screams are made of. Here was the excitement—both physical and aural—that symbolised the rebellion of youth in the ennuied mid-1950's. This was the real thing. Here they were, first five and then four human dynamos generating a beat which was irresistible. Turning back the Rock clock. Pounding out items from Chuck Berry, Little Richard, Carl Perkins, The Coasters and the other great etceteras of the era. Here they were, unmindful of uniformity of dress. Unkempt like long hair. Rugged yet romantic, appealing to both sexes. With calculated naivete and an ingenious, throw-away approach to their music. Effecting indifference to audience response and yet always saying "Thank-you." Reviving interest in, and commanding, enthusiasm for numbers which descended the Charts way back. Popularising (more than any other group) flipside items—example, "Boys". Compelling attention and influencing, wittingly or unwittingly, other groups in the style, choice and presentation of songs.

Essentially a vocal act, hardly ever instrumental (at least not in this country), here they were independently minded, playing what they liked for kicks, kudos and cash. Privileged in having gained prestige and experience from a residency at the Hamburg Top Ten Club during the autumn and winter of last year. Musically authoritative and physically magnetic, example the mean, moody magnificence of drummer Pete Best—a sort of teenage Jeff Chandler. A remarkable variety of talented voices which song-wise sound distinctive, but when speaking, posses the same naivete of tone. Rhythmic revolutionaries. An act which from beginning to end is a succession of climaxes. A personality cult. Seemingly unambitious, yet fluctuating between the self-assured and the vulnerable. Truly a phenomenon—and also a predicament to promoters! Such are the fantastic Beatles. I don't think anything like them will happen again..

ADSVILLE

To promoter Brian Kelly, goes the Adsville Honourable Mention (AHM) for his recent Liverpool Echo jazz column ads about The Beatles at Litherland Town Hall. The name of the group was spelt out in drop capital letters, and arranged in echelon formation. May I say the effect was staggering.

CLOUD 9.

Feeling on top of the world right now are Huyton rocksters Dee Fenton and the Silhouettes. These four friendly fellows have just landed a Friday night-residency at the R.A.F.A. 1250 Beat Club, Bold Street, Liverpool.

Cinecism

Width of screen is no substitute for depth of story!

THE HATE PARADE

The top slot in my parade of disagreeable discs is currently occupied by "The Marcels" treatment of "You Are My Sunshine." Ugh! A record like this one shouldn't even happen once in a Blue Moon!

Bob Wooler's column in the 31 August 1961 issue of *Mersey Beat* was astoundingly prophetic. His positive views of the Beatles proved a talking point around Liverpool – and also intrigued Brian Epstein. Note the Nems advertisement on the same page. The feature appeared a few months before Epstein's alleged claim that he heard about the Beatles only when a boy entered his store asking for their record.

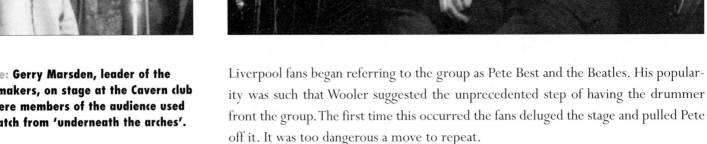

Above: **Gerry Marsden, leader of the Pacemakers, on stage at the Cavern club – where members of the audience used to watch from 'underneath the arches'.**

Above right: **Les Braid of the Swinging Bluejeans and Karl Terry, leader of the Cruisers, during a jam session at the Blue Angel club. Karl was to sing with the Beatles and the Pacemakers in the single appearance by the Beatmakers at Litherland Town Hall on 19 October 1961.**

Liverpool fans began referring to the group as Pete Best and the Beatles. His popularity was such that Wooler suggested the unprecedented step of having the drummer front the group. The first time this occurred the fans deluged the stage and pulled Pete off it. It was too dangerous a move to repeat.

Cavern doorman Pat Delaney was to observe: 'Pete was inclined to be more popular with the girls than any other member of the group . . . girls were attracted by the fact that he wouldn't smile, even though they tried to make him. They also tried to attract his attention on stage, but he wouldn't look at them.'

Rising to the top in Liverpool was no easy task; in the most active rock music scene in the world, more than 350 different groups were performing in the compact area of Merseyside. The Beatles had to compete with a range of groups – Kingsize Taylor and the Dominoes, the Big Three, Rory Storm and the Hurricanes, the Searchers – and the constant challenges tempered their steel.

When Brian Epstein took control of the band, the taming of 'the savage young Beatles' began. He smoothed out the image, made them shed their black leathers, toned down their rock and roll, ordered them not to smoke on stage, to cease swearing, to limit their contact with fans. It was a direction John Lennon loathed, but

OPERATION BIG BEAT

THE HURRICANES RIP IT UP ! . . .
. . . Gold lame shirts included. Johnny Guitar, Rory, Ringo and Lu at New Brighton Tower.

> PHOTOGRAPHS
> IN MERSEY BEAT
> CAN BE
> OBTAINED TO
> ORDER FROM
> THE OFFICE

THE BEATLES IN ACTION . . .   Photo by Dick Matthews
George, Paul, Pete and John, appearing at the highly successful "Operation Big Beat" at the Tower Ballroom. Fans of this popular group will be pleased to hear that copies of their record will be available soon at Nems.

Mersey Beat's coverage of Operation Big Beat featured the two most popular bands at Sam Leach's promotions – the Beatles and Rory Storm & the Hurricanes.

Epstein said that he had to abide by the new rules if he wanted to achieve success. Paul, on the other hand, was delighted with the direction Epstein was leading them.

Yet Pete Best still stood out as the most popular Beatle. When the group appeared on their first radio show in Manchester, he was so besieged by Manchester girls that he had difficulty reaching the group's coach. When the announcement came that the group were signing with Parlophone, it was a solo photo of Pete Best which adorned the cover of *Mersey Beat*.

Suddenly, inexplicably, Pete was called into Brian Epstein's office and told he was sacked. On the very verge of fame, the most popular member of the Beatles had

The Remo Four, one of Liverpool's leading groups, performing at the Cavern. Guitarist Don Andrew was later to form an association of groups called the Mersey Cats.

The Escorts, one of the stable of acts managed by Jim Ireland, on stage at the Mardi Gras club. Its backdrop was a painting of the Liverpool skyline – later, the Star Club was to have a similar backdrop, with a Manhattan skyline!

THE BEST YEARS
OF THE BEATLES

Billy Hatton of the Fourmost – with two admirers sporting beehive hairdos. Formerly the Four Jays, the quartet were a comedy rock band who became part of the Epstein stable and had a series of hit singles, making their debut with Lennon and McCartney's 'Hello Little Girl'.

been thrown out of the group, causing riots among the local fans during which Epstein had to be escorted by bodyguards and George Harrison was given a black eye.

In thirty-five years no satisfactory explanation has been given to Pete Best for this act. In an attempt to excuse what was undoubtedly a cowardly act, Pete Best's ability was unfairly tarnished when Epstein began to encourage a story that he was 'not a good enough drummer'. The majority of musicians and contemporaries of those times dispute this – and many maintain that Pete was actually a better drummer than Ringo.

My own part in the extraordinary events which were to take place began at Liverpool College of Art in 1957. Stuart Sutcliffe and I had become close friends and one day in the college canteen I noticed another student striding by. Dressed in Teddy Boy gear, he was in complete contrast to the other students garbed in uniform polo-neck sweaters and duffel coats. His name was John Lennon.

When John mentioned he had a group, they became the college band. Stu and I, being on the Students' Union committee, arranged for some PA equipment for them to use and booked them for our Saturday night dances.

We met John's two fellow musicians, Paul McCartney and George Harrison, who were studying next door to the college at Liverpool Institute. George and Paul

Right: **Howie Casey and the Seniors
– in a line-up which included Bobby
Thompson, Sam Hardie, Gibson Kemp
and Paddy Chambers. Leader Howie is
at the front.**

would join us in the college canteen and then go up to the 'life rooms' at lunchtime to rehearse.

It was at the Jacaranda club, where John, Stu and I spent many hours, later joined by Paul and George, that I first met their new member Pete Best. I discovered that Pete was a taciturn figure, not as forthcoming in interviews as John or Paul. However, it was soon apparent that he was not only the most handsome member of the Beatles, but he had an aura which appealed to girls. The very fact that he seemed shy or moody was fashionable in the wake of the James Dean image.

By 1960 John, Stu, Paul and George were determined to make their mark as musicians and I conceived a newspaper that would chronicle the exciting events which were happening around us. Having coined the phrase 'Mersey Beat', that was the name I called the newspaper, and it detailed every step of the Beatles' career from July 1961.

I'd discovered an amazing world of hundreds of young rock and roll bands performing in venues stretching the length of Merseyside – crashing out their sounds in cellar clubs and ice rinks, town halls and swimming baths. The vitality was infectious.

It was a marvellous time, an unrepeatable time, when an entire city rocked to the music of youth.

THE BEST YEARS
OF THE BEATLES

1 ▷ BIRTHPLACE OF THE BEATLES

Liverpool, August 1959. Boxing promoter Johnny Best was living in a sprawling Victorian house at 8 Hayman's Green in West Derby village with his wife Mona (known as Mo) and their sons Peter and Rory. Coffee bars were hip at that moment, and Liverpool had its fair share – the Studio, the Jacaranda, El Cabala and the Zodiac among them.

Mo offered Pete and his friends the use of the household cellars as their private club, then decided to turn it into a coffee bar. She named it the Casbah, and hired a resident group to perform – the Quarry Men.

Left: The large Victorian house at 8 Hayman's Green, West Derby, which harboured the Casbah club in its basement. This was the real 'birthplace of the Beatles'.

We have always said that the Casbah was the birthplace of the Beatles. I know that the Cavern in Mathew Street has now announced that it's 'the birthplace of the Beatles', but as far as I'm concerned, it was the Casbah. If it wasn't for the club the Beatles might never have got together again and what happened later wouldn't have transpired.

The house at 8 Hayman's Green, where we lived, was big – big rooms. I used to have a gang of mates come round, school friends, and do what typical fifteen, sixteen-year-olds did at the time – go to the record player, crank it up full blast and play every record you could put your hands on.

Mo, my mother, said, 'Look, you've got cellars underneath, why don't you go down and make it into a den for yourself? It's yours. Do what you want with it.'

So we started working on the cellars with our own little ideas, making fireplaces out of chipboard, putting cork in the ceiling, cleaning it up.

Because of what we were doing, word got out. Coffee bars were the flavour at the time and people started knocking on the door and saying, 'We've heard there's a club going to open.'

Curiosity, plus the fact that there wasn't much going on in West Derby village at the time, meant there was a constant stream of people at the door making enquiries. School friends began to say, 'When's this club gonna open?'

Finally Mo, being an astute businesswoman, said, 'Why *not* make it into a coffee bar?' A great idea. It was all systems go then.

Before, it had been a case of cleaning the room up, scooping the coals out; now there were lights to put in, lots of work to be done. It took on a whole new dimension. When people heard that there was more building work going on, local curiosity came to the boil. A date was set for August, a good time to do it.

Mo came up with the name. We'd been sitting around one day when she said, 'What are we going to call the coffee bar when it opens? You can't just say it's a coffee bar.' Then she came out with the phrase, 'Come to the Casbah' – she said it was something Charles Boyer was supposed to have said in the film *Algiers*.

Mo pointed out that 'everyone will know that expression, or parents will know it', and we sat there and said – 'Wow! Another great idea!' It was our war cry. Everywhere we went, we said, 'Come to the Casbah, come to the Casbah!'

Membership cards were printed and when the word got out, they were all raring to go. At the beginning, it was very much local patronage that started it, but then the club took on such a reputation for itself that people started travelling in from all over Liverpool and the other side of the water, from over the River Mersey. It wasn't in the town centre, it's in a suburb, but we got a fantastic response.

Lowlands was another club in Hayman's Green. It wasn't a coffee bar. They used to have a Sunday night hop with skiffle, then they started to introduce what we called rock bands.

One group who played there was called the Les Stewart Quartet. Ken Brown, one of my school friends from the Collegiate, my grammar school, was a member. So was George Harrison.

Ken had asked Mo about his group having a residency at the Casbah, and she agreed. But Les Stewart refused, so Ken and George left the group and George approached his friends John Lennon and Paul McCartney to set up a band – the Quarry Men. This was a kind of re-forming of an earlier band of the same name.

John Lennon had formed the original Quarry Men as a skiffle group back in March 1957, while he was still attending Quarry Bank school. Lonnie Donegan had brought skiffle to Britain in 1956. Based on an American style of folk music from the 1920s, skiffle swept the country, and thousands of young people formed groups. When the craze began to die down, Liverpool groups turned to rock and roll.

By January 1959, the Quarry Men, whose other members were Paul McCartney and George Harrison, had effectively disbanded. The only member still actively playing in a group was George, who performed with the Les Stewart Quartet. John and Paul still met occasionally to collaborate on songwriting.

Ruth Morrison, George's girlfriend at the time, was one of the many people in the West Derby area to hear rumours of the new coffee bar to open at 8 Hayman's Green, on the opposite side of the road from Lowlands, the club where the Les Stewart Quartet had a residency.

When Mo mentioned to Ruth that she was looking for a group, Ruth suggested her boyfriend's band.

John and Paul captured performing at the Casbah. This photo was the first picture of Lennon and McCartney ever to be published when it appeared in the now defunct *West Derby Reporter*. Enterprising promoter Sam Leach went to the *Reporter* office several years after the photo was shot and bought it for five pounds! The girl smiling at Paul is John's girlfriend Cynthia, later to become his wife. (Sam Leach)

Mo asked to see them and Ken Brown and George visited her. Because of a row with Les Stewart, Ken had left the Quartet, so he and George were free agents. Attracted by Mo's offer of a residency, George contacted his friends John and Paul.

Thus, like a phoenix from the ashes, the Quarry Men — comprising John, Paul, George and Ken Brown — were back in action. They made their debut at the Casbah on Saturday, 29 August 1959 before an audience of 300, and appeared on stage at eight each Saturday evening for a group fee of three pounds. As we'll see, all this changed on 10 October. The Quarry Men left the Casbah — not to return until the following year.

When John and Paul actually came down and met Mo and talked to her about the idea, she said, 'Saturday night. Would you be prepared to open the club?' They said 'Yeah.' And that was the first time I met them.

When they came down, Mo showed them what was happening, where they'd play. There was still painting to be done and so on, so she said, 'Do you want to roll your sleeves up?'

They weren't coerced into it, it was more like a voluntary thing – 'We'll give you a hand.' That's when we had John slapping paint on the ceiling and helping out.

When the four of them began their residency they didn't have a drummer. It didn't really make much difference at the time because other local drummers played on a snare drum with a pair of brushes, so their input was fairly minimal. It was like a throwback to skiffle in a way, but instead of it being a washboard, it was the old snare drum.

The Quarry Men were the first band to play there, so at the beginning no one was saying, 'Hang on, they haven't got a drummer.' It was only later when other bands started to play there and you compared them that it became more apparent. You asked yourself, 'How come that band's got more impact? The Quarry Men are great at vocalising and playing guitars, but with this band, there's a harder beat behind it.' It was a process of elimination; you looked at the groups and suddenly thought, 'Yeah, drums!'

In those days, on a lot of the American records we listened to, the drums weren't prominent. They had drummers who were still playing with brushes or it was just low down in the mix.

Round about the time John, George, Paul and Ken started as resident band at the Casbah, I'd become involved in playing the snare drum and cymbal. My interest in drumming had begun when I'd listened to big band records. This was before rock and roll, of course, and I'd seen some of the early films of that time with Gene Krupa. Krupa, to me, was the epitome of a drummer – you know, big sound.

Then, with the advent of skiffle, the influence of school friends, the opening of the Casbah, and being in a position to actually see groups playing live at the club, I thought, 'Yeah, it would be nice to be a drummer.'

OK, I'd seen drummers before at the Cochran concerts, and all the big stars who came to play at the Empire. Even though I was watching the stars of the shows, I was always concerned about what the drummer was doing. It seemed to be my forte.

When I started listening to music I was also into the habit of knocking beats out with my hands. So people started to say, 'Look, you're playing with your hands.' I'd dabbled with bongos, then friends began saying, 'Why don't you play something?' And when I was asked to play with school friends, they'd say, 'You be the drummer.'

So I used to talk to the drummers who came to the Casbah, asking, 'What's the first thing you do?' They advised the snare drum. The next step was a cymbal. When I mastered the cymbal and the snare drum I thought I was the bees' knees, sitting there.

Then I saw the full drum kits and wanted to move on from snare drum and cymbal. I was becoming more ambitious. That's when I said to Mo and my dad, 'What are the chances of expanding my drum kit?' And they said, 'If that's what you really want to do, we don't mind.'

So we went to see Mr Swift, who was in charge of percussion at that time at the music shop Rushworth's, when it used to be in London Road. He recommended a Premier. 'Good kit, good sound, you would be OK with that.' I looked at it and said, 'When can I come and pick it up?'

My parents signed for it, as they used to do in those days, and Mr Swift said he'd sort out the paperwork. A couple of days later we went down in a taxi to pick it up. Then it was back home to Hayman's and upstairs into the bedroom where I had all my stuff. I set the kit up and it was bang, bang, bang.

That's basically how I got involved with drumming – by watching drummers, plus the fact that people said, 'It's your natural instrument, you have natural rhythm.'

I was playing in my own little band with school friends from the Collegiate in 1959 – the Blackjacks. We were joined by Ken Brown when the Quarry Men threw him out. Why did that happen? It was a combination of things.

Ken suffered from quite severe headaches. On one particular night I think he had a bout of 'flu and wasn't up to playing. He wasn't one of those guys who was sickly or weak and when he wasn't playing he was always at the club. It was like a home from home for him, and he almost became an extension of the Best family – we became that close.

He helped out and did a lot of work at the club and on that night it must have been serious for him not to perform. Mo decided to pay him, even though he didn't play. John, Paul and George then began arguing with Mo, saying that they wanted the fifteen shillings she was going to give to Ken. She said, 'No, I'm not having it, it's going to Ken and that's the end of it.' Of course after that they said, 'We're not going to play here any more.' And Ken Brown had to leave the band.

Initially the Quarry Men were the only band playing at the Casbah, but when they walked out, Mo said, 'Fine, if they're not going to hold that residency down we'll open it up and make sure there's a different band every week.'

Mo started to put on more of the local groups. Soon it was a band every Saturday and Sunday – then Friday, Saturday and Sunday. Then Mo came up with the idea of having bands on every night of the week.

Liverpool youngsters had been exposed to rock and roll through concerts by American rock stars such as Eddie Cochran, who performed at the Empire Theatre on Lime Street, one of the city centre's major venues for concerts.

The Liverpool bands were first known as rock groups, and it wasn't until after the launch of the newspaper *Mersey Beat* in 1961 that they began referring to themselves as beat groups.

It was then that we started to see a lot more of the prominent bands, the likes of Gerry and the Pacemakers, Rory Storm, Derry and the Seniors, the Searchers. So most of the major acts in Liverpool played at the Casbah. It was great because I didn't have to go anywhere to see them. I'd find out who was coming and get to know them and talk to them. I only had to go downstairs and there they were, playing away. Or they'd come upstairs and have a chat, or use the cloakroom. Mo also used the club as a showcase for new talent.

I loved certain bands for their differences. Derry was such a livewire, jumping around – plus the group had Howie Casey on sax. It was a different sound. Then we had Rory Storm and the Hurricanes: an altogether different sound again – and Rory was the ultimate showman. Gerry was more of a rock and roller then, in the early stages of his career. The Searchers became regulars.

Mo liked the music. She was like a teenager. She was very avant-garde for the time.

She'd say, 'You mean this is the new thing, this is rock and roll?' She'd laugh and joke about it, but she liked it and she'd get down there and stand in the crowd when time would allow, watching the bands and enjoying the atmosphere and the foot tapping. She'd go away and have a little dance in the corner.

The incredible thing about it was that there wasn't any alcohol or anything like that. It was coffee, crisps and cola – and the music.

I think we had the biggest delivery in Liverpool of Coca-Cola. It started off when the Coke drivers came with their regular deliveries. They used to roll up with the wagon, pull it down and spend half the afternoon unloading it.

It became like a pit stop for them, you know. They'd go and have a coffee with Mo and a chat – 'How's the club doing?' – and they'd even come to the club. They'd deliver the Coke in the afternoon and then you'd see them with their wives or girlfriends at night.

The clubs and places where rock was played didn't sell alcohol, although we weren't averse to members going out to the pub, as long as they weren't drunk when they came back. Occasionally you'd find the odd small bottle in the toilet that someone had carried in, but it was a rare thing.

The Casbah was, in reality, a coffee bar, so it wasn't licensed. The membership was from the age of sixteen upwards, but we'd sign anybody in above that age and had quite a cross-section of people, including a lot of older people. I mean, we didn't stay open until two o'clock in the morning. It would be something like ten or half past ten.

The police were aware of it and they were very much in favour of the club. They said, 'Yeah, we know it's there; it's doing no harm; it's keeping the kids off the streets and it's giving them an interest; they're entertained, they're behaving themselves.'

In fact, the police used to come down for a cup of coffee like anybody does, to have a laugh and a joke with the family or sit down and say, 'Who's on tonight?'

When the Quarry Men walked out and sacked Ken, he was absorbed into the Blackjacks.

I'd messed about with skiffle with some lads from school, Chas Newby and Billy Barlow. The washboard and that sort of thing at school dances. The little bit of an itch was there, I was quite prepared to stand up and have a go and make some music. Then, when the club opened, it seemed the natural thing because we had the club there and the front rooms to rehearse in.

We said, 'Let's form our own little rock group.' So it was Chas, Billy and myself – and Ken, who was out there playing with the Quarry Men, but joined after the split.

When it came to choosing a name we wanted something we thought was going to sound good. I think we picked it up from an American comic or something.

Blackjack was an old truncheon the Americans used to use – 'Get your blackjack out!' – plus, we'd already thought it would be good if we all dressed in black. When we used to go out we wore black pants and black shirts.

'Blackjacks' seemed to run off the tongue quite well. The name sounded probably better than we were.

We played a couple of times at the Casbah, we did a couple of weddings, we rehearsed a lot.

We were quite proud of playing at the Casbah with the rest of the big Merseyside bands. People saw us playing and word of mouth helped. You know: 'There's a wedding or a birthday party: Blackjacks. They're local.'

At that time we weren't concerned about turning professional. In a way it was a hobby. We liked doing it, we liked the feel of being performers. Ken liked singing, Chas liked singing, so it was fun.

Then the Blackjacks' line-up changed a little bit because Chas went away and studied, he had courses to do. So we had a couple of temporary replacements but still retained the name Blackjacks. Until, that is, I got that fateful call from Paul, which was in August 1960.

Pete Best's group the Blackjacks was in existence for almost a year. Purely by coincidence, the original name John Lennon had chosen for his own group was the Blackjacks, but he changed it after one week to the Quarry Men.

2 ▶ BECOMING A BEATLE

After the Quarry Men abruptly walked out on their Casbah residency, they changed their name briefly to Johnny and the Moondogs and appeared in several talent contests in Liverpool and Manchester. They didn't get together to perform in public again until 14 May 1960, when they appeared at Lathom Hall as the Silver Beats (otherwise known around this time as the Silver Beatles).

I didn't see much of the Quarry Men after they'd walked out of the Casbah. The group wasn't well known in Liverpool, although from watching them I thought they were very versatile at what they were doing. Then they disappeared.

George's brother Peter used to come to the club, and he kept me up to date with what George and the lads were doing. 'Yeah, they passed the Parnes audition, you know, they're up in Scotland backing Johnny Gentle.'

I said, 'That's great, it's happening', but I didn't see them in the same light as Storm, Cass and the Cassanovas, Derry and the Seniors, Gerry Marsden, you know – they were the top dogs, as far as I was concerned.

The Silver Beatles had by now met Allan Williams, an amusing and well-liked character, who ran a popular coffee club called the Jacaranda, in Slater Street. He'd copresented the famous Gene Vincent concert at Liverpool Stadium with pop impresario Larry Parnes, after which Parnes asked him to find some local groups to back his singers, who included Billy Fury. Allan arranged the audition for 10 May 1960 at a club in Seel Street he'd just bought, the Wyvern – later to become the Blue Angel.

The five groups auditioned were Cass and the Cassanovas, Derry and the Seniors, Gerry and the Pacemakers, Cliff Roberts and the Rockers and the Silver Beatles. Parnes chose the Seniors, headed by Howie Casey, and the Silver Beatles. Now a quintet including John's art-school colleague Stuart Sutcliffe on bass guitar and Tommy Moore on drums – a post he held for only two months – the Silver Beatles duly provided backing for singer Johnny Gentle on a Scottish tour from 20 to 28 May, then appeared for the first time at the Jacaranda two days later. Over the next three months, Allan booked them to appear at the Institute, Neston, and the Grosvenor Ballroom, Liscard, across the River Mersey in Wirral.

In Allan's *The Man Who Gave the Beatles Away*, cowritten with William Marshall, many of the Beatles

BEEKAY presents

JIVE AT LATHOM HALL

Every SATURDAY

THIS WEEK — SILVER BEATS, DOMINOES, DELTONES.
7-30 — 11-30.   Admission 4/-.   Members 3/6

FRIDAY TO-NIGHT — Transferred to ALEXANDRA HALL
(L1, L3, L30 to door). 7-30—11 p.m. Admission 3/-

EVERY MONDAY 7-30 — 11 p.m.   Admission 2/6
THIS MONDAY — CLUBMEN

An advertisement for the Silver Beatles' appearance at Lathom Hall. The group actually failed to turn up for the gig as they had joined Johnny Gentle on a short Scottish tour.

myths begin. Take the entries about Stu Sutcliffe. Allan says Stu couldn't play a note and performed with his back to Parnes at the Wyvern audition. This, claims Allan, made Parnes decide not to hire them as Billy Fury's backing group. But Parnes himself said that he was more concerned that Tommy Moore, their then drummer, turned up halfway through the session, was dressed differently from the others, and was quite a few years older than they were. The book's title is a myth in itself: Allan, never having managed the group, didn't have them to give away.

The Blackjacks were still going, although the membership had changed, with Chas studying and Bill doing other things. We did a couple of gigs down at the Casbah and the odd wedding. George still used to come to the club and see me playing drums and maybe he'd talked to the others about me.

So I was still officially a Blackjack when I got the phone call from Paul. I wasn't thinking of going professional or anything like that; I was still just doing it for fun.

I'd left the Collegiate by then and was thinking of going into teaching. It seemed the logical progression – from sixth form to teachers' training college. So all this was still bubbling round in my mind. Still I decided I wasn't going to rush into it.

Then I got the call from Paul and the offer of going to Germany, which was initially for a month. I suppose that changed my outlook a little bit. I wanted to do it, but I also needed to check it out with my parents.

Paul put the deal to me: Allan Williams had booked them for four weeks in Germany. At that time I didn't know where it was going to be, or at which club. They might have known, but I didn't.

The lead-up to the Silver Beatles' offer to go to Germany was convoluted, to say the least. After the Wyvern audition Parnes cancelled his offer to the Seniors, who had given up their day jobs to accommodate him. Allan, confronted by a furious Howie Casey, drove the group to the Two I's coffee bar in Old Compton Street, Soho, in London, where Tommy Steele and Cliff Richard were discovered, in search of work for them. By a remarkable coincidence Bruno Koschmider, a German clubowner whom Allan had tried to interest in Liverpool groups, was in the club. So Derry and the Seniors were the first Liverpool band to make the trek to Hamburg.

Koschmider then asked Allan for more bands. Allan unsuccessfully tried to book Gerry and the Pacemakers and Rory Storm and the Hurricanes before turning, in near desperation, to the Silver Beatles.

But the Silver Beatles lacked an essential something — namely, a drummer. Tommy Moore had left, and his replacement, Norman Chapman, had been conscripted into national service abroad. So when they drifted into the Casbah again, on 8 August 1960, the sight of Pete playing drums with the Blackjacks was decidedly welcome. Soon after they offered him the post in their group, and the chance of going to Germany.

In the event, my parents backed me on the idea of going to Hamburg, saying, 'Yes, it's going to broaden your outlook on life.' They were very forward-looking people. Mo said, 'Anything that's going to be advantageous to you, or broaden your horizons — then do it. I'm not going to keep you cloistered.'

I talked it over with the lads, the Blackjacks. They said that at the end of the day I'd got the offer, and they told me, 'Go. Whether we play again or we don't, it doesn't make any difference to us.' I said that it may only be four weeks, so I might come back and start up again. They said, 'See what happens.'

In the end, of course, the four weeks had spread to five months, and that's why I didn't go back to a job or teacher training college. I decided to persevere with the music.

When I got the phone call they said, 'We've had the offer and we'd like you to come down and audition.' They'd seen me playing drums with the Blackjacks at the Casbah, I suppose it was just to satisfy their curiosity. So they asked me to come down to the Wyvern Club, which later became the Blue Angel, and when I arrived a couple of them were waiting. John was there, George was there, Paul and Stu turned up afterwards.

They said, 'Play six numbers. Do you know this one, do you know this one?' I think we had a go at 'Ramrod', which was a twelve-bar rock and roll piece. It wasn't a problem because what they were playing was very much like what most other bands played. It tended to be a standard repertoire, or you'd heard it so many times on the radio that you could play it. So, yeah, I just blasted them off and while that was going on Allan came into the club, and by that time the audition had basically wrapped.

They were in a corner discussing my performance, and as Allan came up they made up their minds and said to him, 'This is Pete, the new drummer.'

This was the first time I had met him, and when the boys told him they'd made the decision to include me in the band, he said, 'I'm Allan Williams, and I'm the person who's gonna be taking you out. You'll be doing one gig at the Jacaranda so I'll have a chance to see you actually perform and it'll give you a chance to play in my club.'

LATE NIGHT DANCE

BEAT BALLAD SHOW
Presenting
Star of TV and Decca Recording Fame—
JOHNNY GENTLE and HIS GROUP,
Supported by Scotland's Own Tommy Steele—
ALEX. HARVEY and HIS BEAT BAND,
With Ballad Singer—Babby Rankine.

To Entertain and Play For
DANCING
in the
TOWN HALL, ALLOA,
on
FRIDAY, 20th MAY,
9.30 — 1.30.
ADMISSION—Before 10 p.m., 4/-; after 10 p.m., 5/-.

Buses After Dance to the HILLFOOTS DISTRICT.

NEXT FRIDAY. 27th MAY — JOHNNY DOUGLAS and HIS NEW BEAT COMBO with Happy Jackie Benson and Andy Cook of S.T.V.

A local newspaper advertisement for the Silver Beatles' Scottish tour on which they backed Gentle, although the group are not mentioned by name. With the exception of John and drummer Tommy Moore, the members of the band all used pseudonyms: Paul was Paul Ramon, George was Carl Harrison and Stu was Stuart de Stael.

Allan Williams, outside his most famous club – the Blue Angel, one of the most exciting spots in Liverpool. Apart from being the haunt of the Beatles and other Mersey groups, it was graced by celebrities ranging from Judy Garland to Bob Dylan.

I thought, 'Fine.' Then he said, 'It's going to be a rush, so if there's anything I can help you with – I mean, as regards to paperwork or your passport or clearances or anything like that, please let me know.'

I thought what a nice, helpful type of guy he was, very bubbly, you know, laughing and joking. He blew in, and whooooosh – one minute he was there, the next minute he was gone.

So I played with them at the Jacaranda, and that was the only performance I played in Liverpool as a Beatle prior to going to Germany. It was just around this time that the group dropped the 'Silver' from the name.

That Jacaranda gig was the time when we had the mikes tied to broom handles, held by our girlfriends. We played down in the basement and Allan was upstairs that particular night. It was quite an experience because it was totally different from the Casbah as regards coffee bars. I'd never been to the Jacaranda before. I'd heard about it, but this was the first time.

I thought, 'Hang on a minute. I've joined this band which is going out to Hamburg, but here we are playing in the Jacaranda and they're passing mikes around on broom handles. Where are the actual mikestands and stuff? We provide them at the Casbah.'

Then I thought, 'Well, each club has a different atmosphere, a different perspective, who am I to say? It's a one-off gig, we do this and we're off to Germany.' It was good fun, a good experience.

Of course Stuart was playing that night. People still ask me about him. I've always said that Stu knew his own limitations. But with Stuart, the myths spring up and writers fabricate tales, expanding on rumours that he couldn't play with stories about him turning his back on the audience.

In fact, his style of playing meant he held his bass quite high. He was quite small in stature, so he had a prominent position on stage. He had a habit of turning sideways.

I mean, each person develops their own stance. John was a little bit squat and George was very much into tapping his feet.

Stu knew what he had to play and he concentrated a lot on what he had to do. He wasn't as good a bass player as Paul, but what he was doing was good enough for the band. And whatever he did, he gave 200 per cent, and you can't knock him for that.

So this legend that sprang up about him being unable to play the bass is a mystery. You get the impression he stood on stage going dunk! dunk! dunk! It wasn't like that.

Above: The minivan that took the Beatles to Germany being loaded onto the Harwich ferry on 16 August 1960, ready to cross the Channel. Ten people were crammed into the vehicle.
Right: The Jacaranda club as it looked at its reopening in 1984, proudly advertising its Beatles association. The club reopened again in 1996, with Pete Best and his band appearing on the opening night. Although the club's capacity was 150 people, almost 400 crammed into it that night.

THE BEST YEARS
OF THE BEATLES

3 HAMBURG BOUND

The Beatles, as they were now known, set off for Hamburg in August 1960 in an Austin minivan, travelling by ferry from Harwich to the Netherlands, then overland to Germany. Allan Williams and his brother-in-law Barry Chang took turns driving. Also along were Allan's wife Beryl, Lord Woodbine and George Sterner, the group's interpreter.

Sterner, a German waiter, had been working in the Heaven and Hell coffee bar in London. He'd previously acted as Bruno Koschmider's interpreter and wanted to go back to Germany.

Woodbine, from Trinidad, was a well-known Liverpool character who had been associated with Williams in a number of ventures. These included the New Cabaret Artistes in Upper Parliament Street, Liverpool, where the Silver Beatles had been employed to back a stripper called Janice.

On our first trip to Hamburg, we spent a lot of time picking people up. I thought it was going to be a case of Allan simply driving the band out there; but it wasn't to be that simple.

We took the equipment down and loaded the van up. We weren't picked up individually or anything like that. We were told to 'get down there and load up'. There were suitcases and drum kits and, as you can see from old photographs, some of the equipment was loaded on top of the van.

The fact that others would be travelling with us soon became apparent. There was Allan's wife, his brother-in-law and Lord Woodbine. Allan also said, 'I've got to stop off in London en route', and this is when he picked up George Sterner, our interpreter for the trip.

Lord Woodbine – we called him Woody – kept to himself in a way. He tended to be more Allan's honcho. When he was introduced, as Lord Woodbine, everyone fell about laughing, and he played the part. I was intrigued as to how he got the name and

Left: **The weary travellers take a break in Arnhem. John was shopping at the time and George Sterner was also absent. (Left to right: Allan and Beryl Williams, Lord Woodbine, Stuart Sutcliffe, Paul McCartney, George Harrison, Pete Best.)** (Barry Chang)

I asked Allan, 'Hey, not being rude or anything, but how did he get the title?' The two of them started laughing, and he just said, 'It's a long story, another time, another place, I'll tell you all about it.'

But in fact, it wasn't much of a mystery. He was called that because he always smoked that old brand of ciggies called Woodbines.

He was basically Allan's partner. It tended to be Woody and Allan – no pun intended. Woody soon made it clear that he was coming on the trip to have fun.

Beryl, Allan's wife, was quite perky, as she always was. Every time I've seen her she's been quite forceful, chirpy and chatty. She was like that the first time I met her at the Jacaranda and she and Allan seemed well paired. Although she was laughing and joking with the rest of us, she took Allan to task at times, which amused us.

The trip down was very exciting because it was a first major trip out for me. There was the excitement of actually being on the road: something big is happening – we're on our way to Hamburg!

I mean, for everyone the adrenalin was flowing, and there were a lot of high spirits. We had to keep our spirits high because it was such a long trip and we were quite cramped. If you count up, there were us five lads, plus Allan, Woody, Barry and Beryl and, after London, George. So there was the equipment, the luggage and ten people.

In those days, it wasn't a case of just jumping on the motorway. It was A roads and all the rest of it. So the trip was quite long and we did the usual thing, stopping off at transport cafes for a couple of cups of tea or a pie.

Once we'd picked George up in London, we realised that the next leg was from there to the ferry. At the time we didn't realise that Allan was smuggling us out, without permits or anything like that. So when we got to the ferry terminal, he said, 'Now remember, you're students. Leave everything to me, let me talk to the customs people.'

We were naive, you know. We thought, 'He's running the show, let him get on with it. If he wants us to do that, we'll do it.' I don't think we even knew we needed work permits or anything like that, so we were laughing and joking while he talked to the customs people. It was all sorted out and the next thing, we were getting onto the ferry and the van was being loaded on board.

From then on, it was a choice of having a walk round, sitting in the bar for a drink, or being in the cafe. I think the majority of us spent most of our time on deck. We got these little chairs and put overcoats round us and catnapped or kept ourselves amused.

The excitement was still very much there, the bubble. You knew this was an adventure.

The ferry pulled away, and even though we were starting to get tired then, we were thinking that soon we were actually going to be on foreign soil.

Allan said, 'Yeah, we're gonna drive, right the way through to Hamburg.' Then he said, 'I would like to stop off and see Arnhem.' We said, 'Fine.'

At Arnhem, there was time to get out and walk around and stretch our legs. We also went to see the Arnhem war memorial. There are photographs of us sitting in front of it. Seeing the war graves and all the rest of it was quite moving, to me anyway.

It quietened us down a bit. I think it was the aura of the place, the peace and tranquillity that came through to us.

We didn't stay together as a party so while Allan went off to do what he wanted to do, we broke up and did our own things and had a walkabout.

During the walkabout we'd done a bit of shopping. That was when I noticed that John, if he wanted something, wasn't averse to taking it and putting it in his pocket. He said to me, 'This is the way I go shopping. It's a lot cheaper.' So I started laughing, 'Fine, OK.'

On this particular one he dipped for some underpants or something like that. He also dipped a harmonica.

Now a lot of people have asked if that was the harmonica which, a couple of years afterwards, he used on 'Love Me Do'. I wouldn't be able to put my hand on my heart and say it was, because you're talking about August 1960 and 'Love Me Do' came to fruition in April 1962, when we were playing at the Star Club.

But John used it – he was the music for the rest of the trip. Once he got his harmonica, he sat there playing and we were singing the songs and laughing and joking and Allan was singing in his tenor voice. Spirits were high.

John always used to stick it in his pocket, and during that first trip to Hamburg there'd be times when we'd be sitting in the band room at the back of the Bambi Kino, and he'd pull the old harmonica out and play. He'd stick it back in his pocket or throw it on his bed. It was always there. But I don't think that, at that stage, we had any intention of using it on stage. We were just saying, 'Yeah, John, vamp on it, do it!' And he was having fun.

If he'd played harmonica before, I wasn't aware of it. It was quite a surprise to me to see someone take a harmonica out of its case and be quite good at it. The usual thing, when I'd seen someone try to play a harmonica or mouth organ, was the noise

THE BEST YEARS
OF THE BEATLES

The glittering lights of the Reeperbahn in the St Pauli district of Hamburg.
(Pan-Foto/Günter Zint)

of sucking and blowing and a horrendous amount of notes. But John was good, and I thought, 'I've seen this guy playing guitar and I've seen him harmonising. Here he is, giving us a touch of the Larry Adlers.' It was impressive. It was funny, too, because of the faces he pulled when he was playing. He did it just to make people laugh.

John Lennon had learned to play harmonica previously. He was to say, 'I can't remember why I took it up in the first place . . . I know we used to take in students and one of them had a mouth organ and said he'd buy me one if I could learn a tune by the next morning – so I learned about two. I was somewhere between eight and twelve at the time – in short pants anyway. Another time I was travelling to Edinburgh on me own to see me Auntie and I played the mouth organ all the way up on the bus. The driver liked it and told me to meet him at a place in Edinburgh the next morning and he'd give me a good mouth organ. So I went, and he gave me a fantastic one – it really got me going.'

There was that camaraderie and freedom of spirit which helped us along, because it was a long journey.

As we got closer and closer to Hamburg, we had fun. This was the first time we'd encountered trams in the middle of the road. And Allan or Barry, or whoever was driving, was always running into this problem – here we are driving down the road, and the next minute there's a tram hurtling round the corner and it's whoa! Watch out, there's a tram there!

Then we saw the signposts for Hamburg, so we knew it was the final leg. We came in through the middle of the city, the shopping centre. What curiosity! Even though dusk was starting to come down, we had our eyes glued to the window.

We came off what I thought was the main road of the city itself, and then Allan turned round and said, 'The Reeperbahn: we're here.'

As we turned into it, the lights had come on because it was evening by then. It was a massive strip of neon lights which seemed to go on for eternity.

The lights were on on both sides of the road, and there was so much activity going on it was incredible. Those neon lights! It was filled with clubs, bars and people, walking up and down.

We drove down to the end of the Reeperbahn, and Allan shouted, 'There's the Grosse Freiheit, that's where the club is, that's where we're going.' Whoooosh! We drove virtually to the end of the Reeperbahn, turned right and we were in the Grosse Freiheit. We'd seen all the big clubs on the Reeperbahn, then we turned into this little street.

It was tiny compared to the Reeperbahn, but again there was this mass of clubs and neon lights and signs over the road, suspended across the Grosse Freiheit itself. The doormen were touting for business. We had to slow down because there were people walking off the pavement in front of us. We were very close to the strip clubs and could see the advertisements in the windows. It was all, 'Look at that!' and 'What a great place!'

The doormen were in navy blue coats with gold coloured braid, some of them with their hats on so you could identify them. They were outside the different clubs, saying 'Come in for business. Come in for business.' Then we were told, 'That's the Kaiserkeller. That's the club!'

4 ▷ THE INDRA

Derry and the Seniors were already ensconced in Hamburg, at the Kaiserkeller club, when the Beatles arrived in August 1960. Interestingly, when the Seniors' leader, Howie Casey, had heard that Allan Williams was going to send the Beatles to Hamburg, he wrote to Williams pleading with him not to do it because, he said, they were such a bad group they'd ruin things for the other bands. The letter is an indication of how poorly the Beatles were regarded before the Hamburg trip – a judgement that was turned on its head once the band had learned to '*mach shau*' (clubowner Bruno Koschmider's term for 'liven it up').

With a cry of 'That's the club', the band just erupted out of the van. Doors got flung open: the back door, the side door, the front door. People were climbing over the seats and everyone ran down the steps into the Kaiserkeller.

From the top of the Freiheit, you could hear this music piping out, with Derry singing and Howie on sax.

We left Allan in the van and it was just scrambling down the stairs, didn't know where we were going, drawn by the sound of the music and the people, lots of people. And then the doors, opening into the club. It was quite dark. People were dancing and drinking and there was this sound booming out. I was thinking, 'Wow! This is why we're here, this is life!'

We suddenly realised that St Pauli and the Reeperbahn were a red light district . . . open twenty-four hours and full of prostitutes, call girls, transvestites, you name it.

After we got over the initial surge of excitement on the Reeperbahn, we were thrilled to be going into the Kaiserkeller and seeing Derry and the Seniors on stage . . . seeing the type of club, beer being served, people dancing – it was a totally

Left: The Grosse Freiheit, a narrow cobbled street leading off the Reeperbahn. Here the Beatles were to perform at the Indra and Kaiserkeller clubs, and spent much of their leisure time at Harold's bar, watching mud wrestling or visiting the Telefon Bar. (Pan-Foto/Germin)

different atmosphere to anything we'd experienced. We felt like rolling up our sleeves and saying, 'When can we start?'

We thought, 'Oh, it's going to be great playing at the Kaiserkeller', and then, through both Howie and Bruno Koschmider, we found that we were playing at the Indra instead.

Above and opposite: Two shots of the Beatles at the Indra club, ready to 'mach shau'. Pete's outfit is darker than the others as he didn't have clothes to match their stage outfits.

The Beatles were disappointed to find they were booked into a grotty little club, the Indra, at 34 Grosse Freiheit. The group made their debut there on 17 August 1960, and thereafter had to play more than four and a half hours a night. Their sleeping arrangements were far worse than they could have imagined — some dingy rooms at the Bambi-Filmkunsttheater (which they referred to as the Bambi Kino) at 33 Paul-Roosen Strasse.

The Beatles played at the Indra for a total of forty-eight nights, until 3 October. It was during this

period that the group's stage act became much more exciting, and Pete evolved a dynamic new style of drumming that came to be known as the 'atom beat'. Given the difficult conditions, the group's stint at the Indra was something of a baptism of fire.

The Indra was two or three hundred yards down the road, at the bottom of the Grosse Freiheit. We thought, 'Well, if it's like this place we don't mind.' So it was whooosh! down to the Indra. But when we arrived, there were just a couple of people sitting there. It was depressing.

'Why can't we play at the Kaiserkeller?' we asked.

We were told that Koschmider wanted us to try and develop the Indra into another Kaiserkeller.

As time went on it was explained to us by George, the interpreter, who became a waiter at the Kaiserkeller, that Koschmider was a businessman. From his point of view, he had two bands from Liverpool, and he wanted them to build up both his clubs. He felt it was a means of getting the audience to go from one club to the other and back again. Which is what happened.

But at first, we were crestfallen when we saw the Indra. We were also annoyed at being billed as the Silver Beatles and we said, 'We're the Beatles, get it right!'

We were to be shown our sleeping accommodation, and were led across the road. This area was virtually at the bottom end of the Freiheit and there were no lights. Koschmider disappeared. He came back and we saw what turned out to be the exit doors, open. We all looked at one another. Then we went in and found ourselves in a corridor at the back of a cinema.

We passed two dungeons, which turned out to be our bedrooms for many months to come. John, George and Stu got the 'palatial suite'. That was the one with the electric light and the camp bed and the sofa.

The rest of us were looking around, and we said, 'Where are we sleeping? We can't all fit into this one room, there are only three beds and there are five in the band.'

'Two more rooms down there,' we were told. These turned out to be the dungeons. Paul and I were the last to claim our speck, so we ended up there. We were told Allan had been aware of all this and we looked at him and said, 'Is this on a permanent basis or are we just here overnight 'til you get things sorted out?' Allan said, 'Well, I'll talk to Koschmider, we'll fix something up.' But it was something that never got fixed up.

When we first went over to Hamburg we couldn't compare with Derry and the Seniors. On stage, Derry was all over the place, a showman extraordinaire. Howie was rampant with the sax. They were a very active, energetic band. We were quite static. We stood there, playing, while Koschmider watched us and came up with the famous expression, '*Mach schau*'.

He was comparing us with Derry. Because of that, plus the fact that at the time we were playing six, seven hours a night with a fifteen- to twenty-minute break in each hour, we became a band who, all of a sudden, weren't static on stage any more.

We started clowning about. 'If he wants us to "*mach shau*" – "*mach shau*"!' The drumming, stamping our feet on stage, John clowning about, the mock fights, all this was our way of saying, 'All right, if you want us to "*mach shau*" then we'll enjoy ourselves while we're doing it.'

But it caught on, it was very much what the German audience wanted to see.

Also, with the long hours we were playing, we were getting tighter, the sound was getting stronger. We were then starting to play powerhouse music to match Derry's. That just suddenly became the normal thing to do, it became second nature to us.

Koschmider wanted us to play louder – but there was an old lady who lived above the Indra in a flat. This led to trouble.

As our stage act grew, more and more people came to the Indra. Word got out to 'come and see the Beatles', and we were starting to establish ourselves. Derry and the Seniors would be playing at the Kaiserkeller and we'd be playing at the Indra. The Seniors would come off stage and a lot of people from the Kaiserkeller would come down the road to the Indra, watch us, then migrate back to the Kaiserkeller – and so on.

So Koschmider's rubbing his hands. He's got this audience spending an entrance fee to get into one club and an entrance fee to get into the other.

Now, because we were becoming more and more dynamic, and more and more people were coming to the club, this woman upstairs complained. The police came in and had a word with Koschmider. I don't know how many times they'd given him a warning about the noise, but as a result the Indra got closed down.

Koschmider then moved us to the Kaiserkeller, and we started to play alternately with Derry. He'd be on for an hour, then we'd be on, and so on. Then, when Derry went, Rory Storm came.

At one point, when the Seniors and the Beatles were appearing at the Kaiserkeller together, Koschmider had another of his ideas. He stopped playing the jukebox in the intervals, and presented more music. So he split the Seniors into two, and had Stuart Sutcliffe of the Beatles play with Howie on sax and Stan Foster on piano, accompanied by a German drummer.

When Howie recalled those times in a *Mersey Beat* interview, he said: 'The girls used to rave over Pete Best – he was the star boy. He was a great fellow and the one I liked most.'

Despite the undoubted pulling power of Derry and the Seniors, they couldn't hang on at the end of the Kaiserkeller season and wait for the opening of the Top Ten Club. They had to turn down Peter Eckhorn's offer of a season at the new Hamburg club as they'd spent all their money and had to be repatriated.

Further bad luck awaited the group in Liverpool. They were supposed to appear at Allan Williams's new rock and roll club, also called the Top Ten. As we'll see in chapter 10, 'Local Heroes', this club went up in smoke, along with the Seniors' equipment. The group disbanded for a time, then reformed as Howie Casey and the Seniors with Derry and Freddie Starr as vocalists. The Seniors became the first Mersey group to record for a British label when they signed with Fontana and released 'Twist at the Top'.

Clothes were something of a problem. When we first began to play at the Indra, the others had a stage outfit. I think it was a throwback to the Silver Beatles days when they were on tour with Johnny Gentle. They had lilac jackets, a black shirt with a silver stripe on the collar, black pants and crocodile winkle-pickers.

When I joined them, they said, 'We haven't got a jacket that'll fit you.' So they asked what I'd got. I had a black shirt, black pants and an Italian jacket. I seldom played with a jacket, so it was just a case of putting it on and taking it off. I had winkle-pickers, and although they were slightly different from the crocodile ones the rest wore, they said they'd do. So if you see early photographs of the band at the Indra, you'll see them in the lilac jackets and I've got a blue jacket on.

But while we were at the Indra and playing in the jackets six or seven nights a week, it was getting to the stage where they were starting to fall apart. It was sweat. As we became more and more energetic on stage, jackets would get ripped and pants would get ripped and, after a while, we thought, 'What's the point of getting them mended?'

We had Mutti there, the toilet lady, who quite willingly would sew up a jacket or trousers for us in between sessions. She followed us around in our career over there. She went to the Indra, then to the Kaiserkeller, and then when we went to the Top Ten she went to the Top Ten and when we went to the Star Club she ended up at the Star Club too.

She was a lovely old lady, that's why we gave her the name Mutti – 'Mother': a term of endearment. She would say, 'Bring your stuff to me. I'll sew them up.' But it was getting to the stage where each session, we'd go on and she'd stitch them up in the fifteen- to twenty-minute recess, just cobble them together, only to find in the next recess that they'd be hanging off again. She finally said, 'Boys, why don't you throw this stuff away and get yourself something?'

So, because of what we were earning, we started to look at clothes which we could wear on stage as well as on the street.

I've talked about our style of playing as a group. But my own style was evolving too. At the time I joined, the Beatles weren't playing much of their own material. I mean, it was very much standard covers. But it was the variety of their material which impressed me – they were doing Chuck Berry, Little Richard, Carl Perkins, the Everly Brothers, Fats Domino, even some English stuff like Johnny Kidd's 'Shakin' All Over'. I thought, 'Wow! That is something, that repertoire.' And it got even better when we went to Germany. There were certain songs that I played with them which I'd played

Best Wishes
Pete Best

Above and left: Two more shots of the Beatles at the Indra. The leather gear is now beginning to appear, showing that they were wearing leather before their meeting with Klaus Voormann and his circle.

Taking a break between performances: Stu, John, a German friend, George, Paul and Pete with the necessary fortification – beer – on the table!

with the Blackjacks. I'd listened to them and knew the format. It was quite simple in those days: two verses, middle eight, solo, umpty dump and out.

When I rehearsed with the band or practised by myself, if I felt something sounded good I decided to develop it. A lot of it was self-taught, plus I always had in the back of my mind Gene Krupa and his big, powerful sound which carried everything.

In Germany, I was still doing the same thing, but because of the long hours and the fact that we had to develop the music and make it wilder, I began to emphasise what I was doing more. I started slapping the bass drum more to make it a lot stronger, doing more rolls, more cymbal work, and a lot more tom tom work, which was again a throwback to Krupa.

Instead of just playing a single or a double snare drum shot, I started doubling up, so you had this powerful effect. What my right hand was doing on the cymbal, my left hand was doing on the snare drum, basically to emphasise the beat.

So you had stages where it was one bang, one bump bump, and you had that fierce bass drum going on all the time, which was like the backbone to it. So although I wasn't doing anything different from what I'd done before, I felt that this is the way it projected itself and I was developing that particular style.

It seems normal nowadays, but when I brought that back to Liverpool they were saying, 'Hang on a minute, what is this guy doing? What is this "atom beat"?' That's what it was called. I don't know who coined the phrase. Back in Liverpool, drummers of other bands that we were playing with came up and said, 'How the hell do you do that? How do you get that sound? You're doing things which other drummers don't even dream of doing.'

Drummers and other members of bands commented on my style as 'this beat which is booming out and surging everything forward'. I think it was then, when people began to remark on it, that I began to think about it myself. 'What is it that I am doing which is different to them?' Drummers were coming up and asking things like 'How do you keep your bass drum going all the time?' Questions like that stumped me. I thought, 'Doesn't everyone do that?' Then it became apparent, because other people were picking up on it, that maybe there was something special there.

In Germany, when we performed, the others said, 'Crank it up, Pete, we're really going for it tonight.' We played that style right the way through, apart from an early set or late set when we'd coast, we'd sort of take time out and do a couple of slow numbers and fill in and basically relax until the crowds built up – or it was the last set of the night with only a couple of people in, so we'd just play it out.

And of course, when we came back to England and we'd got a situation where we only had to play one hour, it was vooooom! – all of that energy which we'd put into a normal set went into just that one hour on stage. The people listening were just thrown, because everything was so concentrated.

What we were performing was still very much covers, finishing on the big number, 'What'd I Say?' by Ray Charles. We concentrated on getting the audience involved and all that stuff – which had gone down extremely well in Germany. Amazingly enough, it had the same impact on the audiences in England.

5 ▷ STORM

The Beatles kicked off their appearances at the Kaiserkeller on 4 October 1960. Rory Storm and the Hurricanes replaced Derry and the Seniors as the alternate band, and the posters outside the club read: 'Original Rock 'n' Roll Bands. Rory Storm and his Hurican und The Beatles. England – Liverpool.'

When Rory Storm and the Hurricanes arrived, they were given top billing above us on the posters outside the club. I think it was because of their reputation in England.

By this time we'd been in Germany about two months, so I suppose if you look at it from a clubowner's point of view, he's publicising the fact that he's showcasing another new band from Liverpool *and* the Beatles. But when the posters went up, we said, 'Hey, Koschmider, what's going on? We'll blow these guys off the stage.'

I think Rory must have heard that we'd become the top dogs in Hamburg, too. It must have been Howie Casey who spread the news. When Howie went home, he played at the Casbah. My mother told him I'd been writing, but she still asked, 'How are the boys doing out there?' Howie said, 'You will not believe them when they come back home. To coin a phrase: they went out boys and they're going to come back men. They've changed and it's for the good and they're really gonna surprise people.'

So Mo wrote that big things had been said about the band. Rory must have heard about the change, too.

Rory Storm and the Hurricanes were one of the top bands in Liverpool at that time. Very professional, with very slick routines. It was great for Koschmider because he got rid of one showman and got another back in.

Even though they were billed over us, on the musical front we were still the top dogs. The Hurricanes were getting a good response, people liked them . . . if they didn't like them they'd show it, it was that simple. Yet we were still the ones who were

Left: All the Mersey groups liked to get up to high jinks on stage and the Hurricanes were no exception. Here drummer Ringo Starr fools around with a guitar. (Cavern/Mecca)

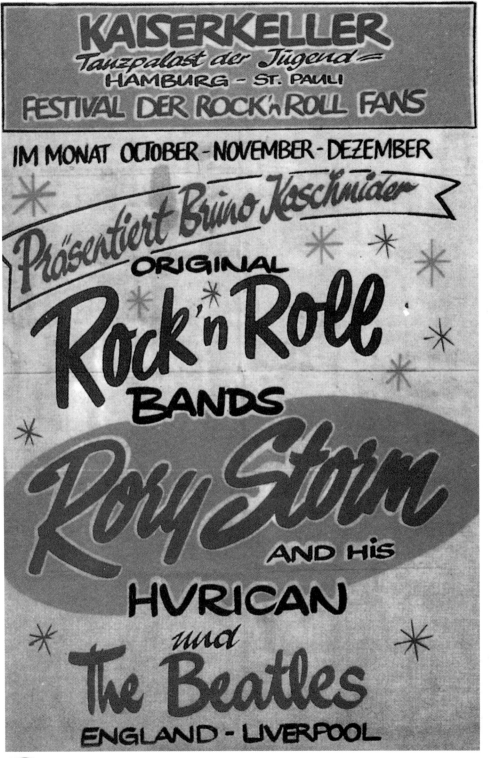

bringing the house down. It was good because there was a camaraderie there. We grew very close, which happens with bands when you're away from home, living under the same roof together and playing in the same club. It was interesting that there was also a very friendly rivalry, if I can put it that way. Especially on a Saturday night, which was the big night.

We'd laugh and joke about it with the other band. You know: 'We'll blow you off the stage tonight. You go out and do your best bit, go on, see what you can do and we'll still come out and take you to the cleaners.' 'Oh no you won't.' And so on. It was just banter but it added to the excitement and the atmosphere and the German audiences were electrified by it because we came up with things to outdo one another. We were all enhanced by the competition — word was out and the audiences were getting bigger.

Even while Derry was there, there were people who just came to see the Beatles. We had our regular following at the Indra and when we went to the Kaiserkeller we had a combination of both of them.

This is where the truth differs from the legend again. These days, the image people have of those days are of an audience that was always made up of drunken sailors and troops. It wasn't. It

Left: Liverpool's 'golden boy', Rory Storm, in action. Dubbed 'Mr Showmanship' by Cavern DJ Bob Wooler, Rory was also called 'the king of Liverpool'. He was a bigger name in Liverpool than the Beatles at the time. (Cavern/Mecca)

Far left: This hand-painted poster announced the Hurricanes and the Beatles at the Kaiserkeller. Johnny 'Guitar' Byrne of the Hurricanes, following an argument with Bruno Koschmider, decided to take it as a souvenir – and so saved it for posterity!

tended to be regular German people who came out to listen to the rock and roll bands, dance, enjoy themselves, get drunk. As to the violence, I suppose it depends on which way you look at it. If you're brought up in that environment, then it probably doesn't seem as violent.

We'd never seen violence to the extent where there are fights in clubs with waiters throwing drunks out and gas guns, pocket truncheons, that type of stuff being used.

The Hurricanes lived as well as performed at the Kaiserkeller. We felt that we'd been done out of it. We knew that Derry and the Seniors were stopping at the Kaiserkeller, and thought we'd move in when they left. It would have been dead handy, the rooms and the living quarters. But we were told, 'No.' Rory moved in and took over there. We were still in the Bambi Kino.

But I think that we probably utilised the rooms at the Kaiserkeller just as much as they did, apart from sleeping in them. We used to use those rooms in between sets, we'd flop down in there and drink beer when they went on stage – so apart from it being the place where they slept at night, it became something of a communal room.

Rory Storm – I loved him. I liked him as a performer and I liked him as a person. I was fortunate because he was one of the first bands who came to the Casbah, and I got to know him as a friend and as a performer through the intimacy of the club.

One night I was playing with the Blackjacks and I bet him that we'd draw more than he would. It was all friendly banter, and I think the bet was massive – like a shilling!

We played and pulled in about 400. When they were next on, Rory was there as the crowd was coming in, saying, 'Are you keeping an account of this, Mo?' All good humoured stuff. He walked off down to the gate, and was saying to people passing by, 'Come on, get in and see the show.'

I know at the end of the night we flipped a coin and he laughed and said, 'Buy me a Coke.'

Rory was always a great showman, an extrovert, and the funny thing was he had this terrible stutter offstage, but on stage he was OK. At the stadium show where I saw him for the first time, he created such an impression.

The stadium was a second home to me. I'd been there as a kid watching the boxing bouts, what with my dad being a promoter, but it was quite different to be sitting watching a rock show going on in the ring.

At this show, the music started, Storm was announced, the Hurricanes came on stage. The music kept going on and on. Pow! Pow! But where the hell was Rory? It kept on going. Finally he picked his moment and walked down from the back of the hall where the boxers used to come from. In his gold lamé suit, with that blond hair of his, he cut a very impressive figure – the classic showman.

He took his time walking down; the crowd's adulation meant he had to go slowly. Then he jumped into the ring and went into his number.

I was sitting there and I thought to myself, 'That's great.' He basically stole the show with his entrance.

Rory lived for rock and roll. His real name was Alan Caldwell, but he changed it by deed poll to Rory Storm and renamed the family home in Broadgreen 'Stormsville'.

Rory also devised Western-sounding names for the members of his band – a reflection of the popularity of TV westerns at the time. (He called his first band 'Al Caldwell's Texans'.) He dubbed Walter Eymond 'Lou Walters', although friends still referred to him as Wally. Although he was the group's bass guitarist, he also sang several numbers and had a distinctive voice – certainly a better voice than Rory's, although Rory was a magical stage performer.

Guitarist Ty Brian was named after Ty Hardin and Johnny Byrne, one of Liverpool's premier lead guitarists, was dubbed Johnny Guitar, after the Joan Crawford film of the same name. Rory gave drummer Ritchie Starkey the name Ringo Starr – and even provided him with his own solo spot called 'Ringo Starrtime'.

Rory Storm and the Hurricanes appeared on numerous bills with the Beatles in Liverpool and were teamed up together more times than any other band in those early days, which is possibly why the Beatles chose Ringo to replace Pete – he was somebody they were very familiar with.

Beatle scribes often make out that the Beatles only became familiar with Ringo in Hamburg, intimating that they chose him because he was such a good drummer. The decision was more likely to have been made because the two groups had forged such a firm friendship.

Both Rory and Ty were to suffer tragically early deaths, and what ultimately emerges from the Rory Storm story is that the wider world never had the opportunity of enjoying the performances of one of Liverpool's most distinctive bands.

Later, when Rory came to the Casbah, I got to know them all: Lou – or Wally, whichever way you want to call him – Ty, Johnny, Ringo, and they were all laughing and joking, and it just went on from that. We played an awful lot of bills together at a lot of different venues.

At the Kaiserkeller we'd been having problems for a long time with the stage. If you stamped on it or bounced on it or something like that, it went boooooiiiing! Like

Lou Walters, the Hurricanes' bespectacled bass guitarist/vocalist, took to the stage and sang with the Beatles at the Indra. Allan Williams wanted to make a record with him and booked a tiny studio near to the main railway station on 15 October 1960. Accompanying him on the number 'Summertime' were John, Paul, George – and Ringo Starr, playing with the three for the first time.

The Liverpool groups used to socialise at clubs and parties. Here, Hurricanes drummer Ringo relaxes with the Beatles at a party. (Cavern/Mecca)

a springboard. Koschmider kept promising, 'Yes, I'll get it fixed for you.' But it got so bad that the only way to get him to fix it was to destroy it first.

So we talked this over with Storm, and both bands introduced the stomp as part of the show. We said that if we persisted with the stomping on stage, the stage is gonna go, it's as simple as that.

We were having bets among ourselves on which band was going to do it. We'd try to bust the stage during our sets, but it hung on and we were getting frustrated.

We were in Harold's Cafe, across the road from the Kaiserkeller. The next thing we knew, Rory came running over the Freiheit, followed by the Hurricanes. It was all jubilant laughter and shouts of 'We've done it, the stage has gone down! We've cracked it!' We thought, 'Oh, great', and asked what was happening at the club. Rory said, 'Oh, they're just propping it up again. It's all busted, dipped down, caved in. So that's why we're off and you're back on again next.'

When we went back on the stage to perform, it had in fact been propped up with empty beer crates and stuff wedged in to keep it up. As we walked on, it was just like a waterbed. When the stage had gone down, the drum kit had sort of caved in to the middle and we thought, 'This is it, we can't play on this any more. We've achieved what we wanted to do.' But all Koschmider did was reinforce it, so we ended up still playing on this grotty stage.

They threw Rory out because of this, and they wouldn't let him stay in the changing rooms at the Kaiserkeller. The Hurricanes and us went to Koschmider and said, 'Hey, come on, what's going on? You can't throw him out in the street. He's got nowhere to sleep and you can't treat people like that.' Eventually he let Rory come back, but it took quite a lot of persuading.

Some of the Beatles joined some of the Hurricanes for a recording, paid for by Allan Williams, at the Akustik studios at 57 Kirchenallee, in Hamburg, on Saturday, 15 October 1960. This was basically a record-your-voice booth behind the Hamburg rail station. John, George and Paul actually backed Lou Walters on 'Summertime', and then Ty Hardin and Johnny Guitar joined Lou and Ringo on 'Fever' and 'September Song'. The three Beatles then asked Allan if he would let them record a few numbers, but he refused.

There were several copies of this disc. Allan lost his copies when he left them behind in a London pub. Rory Storm and Lou Walters had copies, but Rory's seems to have vanished and Lou gave his copy to his ex-wife.

Rory Storm was the front man of the Hurricanes, but Wally used to sing numbers like 'Fever' and 'Summertime', and those songs used to go down well. So Allan wanted to record Wally, and got the idea of bringing in the three frontline Beatles for the harmonising. He kept Ringo as drummer, because he played 'Fever' and 'Summertime' with Wally all the time. 'Fever' is one of those numbers which you need to be familiar with to play, although the chord sequences of all the rest of it weren't hard to get to grips with.

I think Allan realised at the time that a strong aspect of the Beatles' work, apart from the energy which they'd evolved, was the harmonising. They were doing very good harmony work, so Allan came up with the idea of Lou — who Allan regarded as a better singer than Rory — singing.

Why at this stage would Allan think of just three of the Beatles? I suppose he didn't pick Stu on bass because Wally was a bass player.

I suppose another way of looking at the venture was that it was another of Allan's off-the-wall ideas. At that stage no one asked 'Why is he doing it?' As it happens, it didn't cause any splits in the band or anything. Rory was aware of the fact that Wally was doing the recording and we were aware of the fact that John, George and Paul were on it.

KAISERKELLER DAYS

Starved of English food, the Beatles soon discovered a solution in the Seamen's Mission via Iain Hines of the Jets, the first British rock group to be booked into Hamburg. Jim Hawke, a former British serviceman, and his German wife Lilo ran the Mission in those days.

Hawke liked the Beatles and let them have meals on the cheap. This was necessary, as they were always broke at the time. Bruno Koschmider's contract with the group offered them 30 Deutsche Marks each a day for playing four and a half hours on a weeknight and six hours on Saturdays and Sundays. There was also a clause forbidding the group to play at any other venue within a radius of twenty-five miles.

Socially, the Beatles ricocheted between Harold's Cafe, across from the Kaiserkeller, and the Seaman's Mission. They attracted as much attention off stage as on for their boisterous and unruly, often outrageous, behaviour.

We discovered the Seamen's Mission. When we got up, which was more or less in the middle of the afternoon, food was usually high on the agenda. But we were getting fed up with German food, which was all we could really get in the St Pauli area: sausages, bratwurst, that type of stuff. It wasn't quite what we wanted.

We wandered off to the harbour one day because people had said we might be able to get English food down there, at the Seamen's Mission. When we found it, and discovered that the people who were running it were English, we asked, 'Got any cornflakes?' And they laughed. Young rock musicians, all dressed in leathers and cowboy boots, wanting cornflakes.

Jim Hawke, who ran the Mission then, said he didn't have them readily available and we told him that if he got them for us we'd come down there regularly. And that's where we used to go to have our cornflakes and steak, egg and chips, our staple diet. That's how the Seamen's Mission became famous for feeding the Beatles.

At night, when the Seamen's Mission was closed, we'd go over the road to Harold's Cafe. We'd get chicken soup or sausages or whatever Harold had on the menu. The cafe was a good meeting point. We tended to use it as a meeting place when the Mission was closed, but in the mornings, we'd always head off for the Seamen's

Left: George, Stu and John look suitably solemn as they pose for Astrid in Hamburg in November 1960.
(Astrid Kirchherr/Redferns)

Mission, and we told Ringo and his gang about it and took them down there. They were the new lads in town.

We used to do crazy stuff, like fighting in the street. We held traffic up on the Reeperbahn once, pretending to fight – just running around shoving one another and kicking, walloping backsides and all that type of stuff, but doing it in such a way that it looked quite serious. Because of that the police warned us that if it happened again they wouldn't look lightly on the situation.

Poor old Harold. When we came in to his cafe he'd be sitting down and would put his hands up to his head. He was a big fella, but he felt it. He was probably thinking, 'Oh my God, here they are again', or 'What is going to happen now?'

The usual thing would be for us to start with the bread rolls, throwing them at one another across the tables. When we got away with that we became more ambitious, with chicken wings or chicken legs or spaghetti. Someone would be sitting there and a plate of spaghetti would land in their lap, or one of us would pick up the spaghetti and put it on their head.

And then there were the beer fights, with bottled beer.

Harold's Cafe must have been like a battleground sometimes, with Storm's mob and our mob there. There were many times in there, after we'd done a long session, when we'd meet and do the usual; shake the beer up, and spray it across the table! Often there were eight guys in there all spraying their beers around, plus whoever else came with us to keep us company.

We'd usually be at the back of Harold's Cafe, a part shaped like a horseshoe. There'd be all this mayhem going on at the back here, and Harold would be at the front trying to run his business and keep an eye on us. He was quite good-humoured about it at times, but sometimes we left the place pretty near destroyed.

At the fleamarket, throwing things from stall to stall, we started a riot. We took stuff from one stall, put it on another stall. We got the vendor from one stall arguing with another vendor, saying, 'What are you doing with my stuff?' We planted it there and then we'd take stuff and throw it as we were walking, over the top of the stall.

There was one particular occasion, on a Sunday morning, when we caused so much mayhem that it was like a free-for-all going on among the vendors. Then we went off to the bar on the other side of the fleamarket and were sitting there, watching this riot we created going on. People pushing one another, falling over the stalls with the public standing around gaping. The police wagon was called up and we were sitting there watching it all through a drunken haze, still drinking away in the early hours of the morning.

The thing about it was that no one gave a damn. No one worried about it, no one came back and said, 'Good God, what have we done?' It was just, 'So what?' We had a good laugh about it.

A lot of people have said it could have been the boredom factor and long hours – but it wasn't. That tended to be our excuse. Actually, it was what we could get away with. And then we'd say, 'Let's try another.' It was a lot of fun at times.

We sometimes got into real fights.

Howie Casey and Gibson Kemp at the Blue Angel. Although initially unimpressed by the Beatles, Howie was pleasantly surprised at their development in Germany and sang their praises back home. Gibson, who replaced Ringo in the Hurricanes, married Stu Sutcliffe's former fiancée, Astrid Kirchherr.

There were people who, because we were English and, I suppose, because of the long hair and our general attitude, took a dislike to us. There were some who could get quite ugly towards the Beatles. They'd swear at you, say, 'Stupid, bloody Englishmen', that type of stuff.

We'd usually just swear back at them, 'Bugger off, you stupid git', and continue doing what we were doing. But there were times when we knew they would take the initiative. They'd start pushing and shouting at us. We'd seen street fights before so, yeah, there were times when we were involved in fights. John was involved in a couple of fights, and I think Paul had people shoving him. It always tended to be when the German waiters weren't around to defuse the situation.

If people spoiling for a fight saw us on our own, that was when it would happen. If they saw a couple of waiters with us, they knew that if they said anything, the waiters were going to defend us, which they did. The waiters would be the first to tell us if someone was saying something in German which we didn't fully understand. They'd be the first to finish it or say, 'I'll deal with it.'

Still, the times when we were hustled we gave as good as we got . . . and I think that surprised a lot of people. I think most probably they thought, 'Here they are, the lads from Liverpool, silly Englishmen. Because they're musicians they won't be able to fight.'

But most people in Liverpool at that time, because of their upbringing, could handle themselves to a degree. We wouldn't walk away from it. We'd try and stop it, but if a fight did start then we'd get stuck in, we'd be prepared to have a go.

Klaus Voormann, the son of a Berlin doctor, had been studying in Hamburg since 1956. Astrid Kirchherr was his girlfriend. After the two quarrelled one night, he was walking through the St Pauli district and entered the Kaiserkeller, attracted by the sounds of Rory Storm and the Hurricanes. He was entranced, however, by the Beatles, and he began to bring Astrid and his other friends along to watch the band.

Klaus Voormann came to the Kaiserkeller to see us and brought along his girlfriend Astrid and other friends. We called them the 'exis'. It was short for existentialism, which was fashionable at the time. Everyone who didn't fit into the normal pattern was an existentialist.

It wasn't that they didn't readily mix with everyone else; they tended to stand out, not because they flaunted it and said, 'Here we are', but because of their style of dress, which differed from the run-of-the-mill people. It was all black tee shirts, polo-neck sweaters, leather jackets. It's said that they had a big influence on the Beatles. A lot of people say a lot of the Beatles' style was created at that particular time.

I tend to think it was a combination of things. We wore leathers because we liked leathers, and leathers were cheap over there. Leather was hardwearing, and we could use it on and off stage.

So I wouldn't say that our style was because of the 'exis'. I mean, they had no musical influence, but their style of dress did appeal to us. John was arty, Stu was still arty, and I suppose in our own way we wanted to look a little bit different. You could get that type of clothing over there, it was readily available, more so than in England. So it was a natural progression for us to get the black clothes.

As for the leather jackets, we got them when we were still at the Indra. When the lilac jackets started to fall apart, we went to the C&A in the Reeperbahn and got some semi-blouson bomber-like jackets, very American-looking, in a dogtooth check. They had white and black and red and black with the collar buttoned up. By this time we were knocking round in jeans anyway; they were cheap. So we said, 'We'll get them, we'll get a red one and a white one, then we can chop and change.' We saw flat pink caps too, so we all decided we'd wear flat hats on stage.

But we became more and more aware of the fact that we could afford to get leather, and we found the shops where we could get it quite cheaply.

The waiters used to wear leather jackets, the same type we went for. George went out and got one and then, when we saw it, we followed suit. Paul was the last to get one, while Stu didn't get one at the time.

We decided to use the leather jackets for knocking about. But gradually we began to get sick of wearing the C&A jackets on stage. We felt we looked stupid in them. We began to wear jeans, polo-necks on stage – playing in what we were standing in.

And the cowboy boots. We said, 'We're gonna get cowboy boots because we like them.' Plus, they made us feel taller than anyone else.

So our style wasn't planned, it was something which evolved. It wasn't like we said, 'We're all going to get leather jackets and we're all going to get cowboy boots and we're all gonna wear polo-necked sweaters.' We found that you could eat, sleep, drink, do whatever you wanted to do in what you played in on stage.

Later, when we were at the Kaiserkeller, we saw Astrid wearing a very expensive leather jacket and leather jeans, and suede outfits. When Stu got involved with Astrid he bought a leather jacket that was a lot more expensive than ours were.

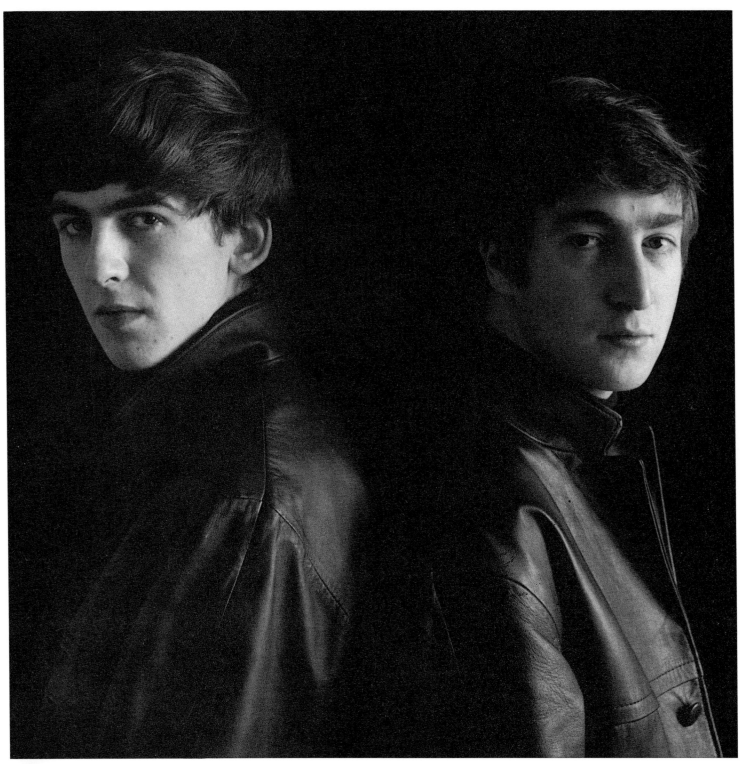

THE BEST YEARS
OF THE BEATLES

7 ▶ ASTRID

Astrid Kirchherr, Klaus Voormann and Jürgen Vollmer were all, for different reasons, vital to the Beatles' evolution. Astrid is famous for her tragic romance with Stuart Sutcliffe; Klaus was the first of his group to see the Beatles, and later became closely associated with them as a bass guitarist; and Jürgen, like Astrid, took some classic early photographs and helped develop their hairstyle.

Astrid was a student living with her widowed mother in Altona, a suburb of Hamburg. Although she was with Klaus when she first saw the Beatles, she fell in love with Stu. Stu then moved into the attic room of her home, after Klaus had vacated it.

As I've said, Klaus had been an admirer for some time. He'd seen us play, he watched from afar. Then he came down with Astrid and other people. They watched the band and were completely enthralled by the image, the antics on stage and the type of music we were playing. I think Klaus spoke to Stu first – then we were all introduced.

By then the love story had already started for Stu. Stu was besotted with Astrid, he would always keep an eye out for her and the minute that she was there, he was very intense and playing specially for her. It was then that he started playing 'Love Me Tender'.

He'd played it a few times before, but now it was more intense, because of Astrid. I suppose it was Stu's way of serenading her. He insisted that it had to be done when she was in the audience, and he used to take a lot of stick for it. I suppose we could be quite cruel sometimes, inasmuch as we'd say, 'Astrid's in the audience, it's "Love Me Tender" time, come on, get it over and done with', that type of stuff. But he took it in good humour.

Astrid began to take photos of the group – which led to another aspect of the Beatles legend.

Her photos of the Beatles at the time give the misleading impression that I was a loner. You have all these photographs, but apart from the Dome shot, taken at a fairground in a park in Hamburg, there is nothing else of me. There are portraits of

Stu Sutcliffe in one of a number of photographs by Astrid of the Beatle she loved. Stu's life altered when he met the blonde-haired German student and he was to leave the Beatles and enrol at the State High School of Art Instruction in Hamburg because of her. Tragically, he was to die in Astrid's arms on 10 April 1962. (Astrid Kirchherr/Redferns)

John, George and Stu, of George, John and Paul on the roof in cowboy boots and leathers and so on.

What people fail to realise is that there were times when I *had* to be elsewhere. It was something along the lines of, 'Yeah, we're going to see Astrid, but you're the drummer, you've got skins to go and get, sticks to buy and you've got to go into town to do it because there's nothing here.' So I'd be away for an afternoon.

But when she said, 'It's a group shot, I'd like to get everyone', like the Dome one, we were all walking around with her. But there were other times when she'd taken them while I was away, not through my choosing. It was not as if I was saying, 'I'm not having my photograph taken.'

The photographs Jürgen later took of the Beatles at the Top Ten club are as historically important as Astrid's. In Jürgen's photographic portfolio, published as *Rock 'n' Roll Times*, Pete is once again conspicuous by his absence. The photographs were taken during a performance and concentrate on the Beatles' front line.

Astrid is usually credited with creating the Beatles' 'moptop', but a number of influences shaped the hairstyle. In *Rock 'n' Roll Times*, Jürgen was to recall the occasion, in September 1961, when John and Paul visited him in Paris. 'John and Paul . . . decided to have their hair like mine. A lot of French youth wore it that way. I gave both of them their first "Beatles" haircut in my hotel room on the Left Bank.'

As for the story of Astrid and the Beatles' hair – this didn't happen on the first trip. Stu was the first to have the style; at the end of our first stay in Germany, Stu

Astrid outside the Cavern club during an under-sixteens session in 1964. After Stuart's death she made several trips to Liverpool and fell in love with the city and its people. She was to capture it all through the lens of her camera and in 1995 a portfolio of photographs was published in her book, *Liverpool Days*.
(Max Schleler/Redferns)

The relationship between Astrid and John was very close. When she visited Britain in 1964 the Beatles welcomed her with open arms. (Max Schleler/Redferns)

had stayed on in Hamburg, Paul and I were deported, and then John followed on because he was dispirited and didn't like what was going on. But when we went back to the Top Ten, Stu was the first to start to wear his hair down. The first thing John, Paul and I did was to go and get measured up for leather pants again. This time it was not going to be the stuff you could buy in the shops, we were going to get tailor-made leather pants, good quality leather, lined and all the rest of it.

Then Stu came in with his hair combed down. Astrid had done it. At the time we were still wearing our hair swept back, so he took the usual stick – 'What are you doing? Put your hair back.' He combed it up. Then, lo and behold, he'd combed it down again the next time he came in. It got to the stage where he started wearing it like that all the time.

The next to follow suit was George. Then after we came back to Liverpool from the Top Ten, John and Paul went to Paris on holiday, where they met Jürgen. And when they came back from Paris a couple of months after the Top Ten, they had their hair in this style.

By the time John and Paul had come back from Paris, Stuart had left the band and decided he was staying in Hamburg, at art college. So it left the other three and myself. But no one actually said, 'Comb your hair down.' I mean, I'd have done it. I'd followed suit with everything else: the leather jackets, the cowboy boots, growing my hair long, that sort of stuff. It wasn't a case of not conforming; it was just the fact that it didn't seem to be important at the time.

8 ▶ IN ST PAULI

The infamous St Pauli district of Hamburg was one of the most celebrated red light districts in Europe. The effect such a place had on four young lads from Liverpool can be guessed.

In Liverpool, striptease clubs were banned by order of the Watch Committee – despite which Allan Williams and Lord Woodbine managed to run such a club for several weeks – and pub opening hours were very restricted. There were many periods during the day when it was also impossible to buy alcohol in Liverpool. St Pauli, by contrast, had bars open twenty-four hours a day, was crammed with strip clubs, and presented a variety of sex shows in some of its clubs, mainly centred around the notorious Reeperbahn.

Yet the area wasn't as dangerous or violent as it is often pictured. True, waiters used strongarm methods on difficult and drunken clients, and there were numerous gangsters, but it was also an area visited by families and young people. There was a police station on the Reeperbahn and a church in the Grosse Freiheit, directly opposite the Kaiserkeller. Youngsters under eighteen had a ten o'clock curfew.

Left and following pages: **When the Beatles were in Hamburg they engaged in a great deal of horseplay, both on stage and off. Their Goonish humour, apparent in John Lennon's writings and Paul McCartney's letters, was also evident in these photographs. The tales of them appearing on stage with toilet seats round their necks or walking along the Reeperbahn in their under-pants are confirmed by photographs taken at the time. The first shows a bowler-hatted Paul on a lavatory in a dressing room. Next, Paul and John loon for the camera, with Paul's underpants on show; while in the third it's John's turn to display his underpants – appropriate in an area with a thousand strippers.** (Hunter Davies)

Once we'd established ourselves, the girls began to appear. It wasn't a case of playing one night, and the next day the girls were flocking through the back doors. But once they warmed to us, they liked us, and wanted to get to grips with us. They found out where we were staying because there were times when we'd finish what we were doing, go for a meal, drinks and so on, and stagger down the Grosse Freiheit. They would see us going through the back door of the Bambi Kino and say, 'Ahhhhh! So that's where they're staying.'

We had the keys to those doors, though. If we didn't want to open the doors, no one could get in. But they found that they could come in through the cinema, and go through the side and along this corridor which led from the back where the toilets were. We used to wash in the toilets, and there'd be many times when we'd stagger in there and there'd be girls already in there for us. They'd found a way in, so we'd think, 'Ah well! Here they are, may as well enjoy ourselves' – or there'd be times when we'd just turn round and say, 'Oh no, get out. Go!' Just kick them out again.

I'm not trying to paint a picture of every girl in the St Pauli area being ready to give themselves to the Beatles. There were girls with whom you might get there in the

end, but they weren't readily going to do it on the first night: but within the audience some were high-class call girls, and sometimes they'd take a fancy to you, quite openly. They'd send a waiter to say, 'Tell him I like him and I want to go to bed with him.'

Sometimes they'd buy you presents: gold bracelets, a gold chain, a lighter or whatever, to show their affection. The problem with that was they then thought you were theirs; it became very difficult to break favour with them, and if you did, they had no time for you at all.

I would say, 'Hello' to them and they wouldn't want to know me. Or, one of their favourite tricks: if you'd broken up, then they'd come in with another guy, or even a member from another band, and blatantly sit in front, all over them, trying to arouse your jealousy. With some people it worked – others it was water off a duck's back.

We did have girlfriends, but I wouldn't call them steady girlfriends. I mean, there were too many, and we played the field too fast and furious. There were some we spent time with a little bit longer, but we certainly weren't one-girl people.

Sometimes you'd finish with one of them, but they would press themselves on you again, so you'd pick up the relationship. It was a case of, 'I'll see her at seven or eight after the club, but while I'm seeing her I'll arrange something with someone else.' There was so much on offer, we didn't want to tie ourselves down.

We were also told about the Herbertstrasse. One day one of the waiters said, 'Oh, haven't you seen the girls in the shop windows? In Herbertstrasse.'

We found it and looked at it in amazement, walking up and down the street five or six times just staring at these people. But then we actually got to know some of the girls who used to be in the windows – in their time off, they'd be at the show at night, even though it was sometimes hard to recognise them with their clothes on.

We'd spend many pleasurable hours just window shopping, as we called it. We had nothing to do so, yeah, we'd walk up and down the Herbertstrasse, laughing and joking, playing pranks, looking at the girls. Not that we did any business with them. If we wanted to we could do it in our own time when they were off duty. But it was just like a nice stroll to go past them, and soon they began to recognise us. 'Yeah, it's the Beatles in Hamburg.'

There was a time when we attempted to mug a seaman. It wasn't because we were born convicts or had criminal tendencies or anything like that. Far from it. We went out to Hamburg as seventeen-, eighteen-, nineteen-year-olds. The money that we were on was OK, twelve or fifteen pounds per week. I suppose to us at that time it seemed an awful lot of money. But when we were over there, we blew our money, as youngsters will do. As well as having to live on it, drink on it, eat on it, we had to buy instruments with it. You'd be paid on Thursday and by Friday or Saturday you'd be broke or you'd just have a couple of marks left in your pocket.

It often came down to this: 'I need that cash and what's better, a pair of socks or a bottle of beer?' A bottle of beer! That was our outlook on life. It got to the point where we'd survive, but we didn't have a lot. Then John and I got this harebrained bloody idea in our heads.

People were always hospitable to the Beatles and we could get drunk without having to pay for it. There were so many beers bought for us, schnapps and champagne. On this particular night a sailor had come into town, loved the band and had bought us loads and loads of booze on stage. He came up afterwards, said he wanted to take us out for dinner. He was paying for it, so we went out and ate. John and I were sitting there, with Paul and George. And this guy had a real big wad. I mean, he must have just been paid off or something like that. It was one of those things that looked like a house brick by the time you opened it up.

We were full of drink and saying, 'Wouldn't be a bad idea if we tried to get that, split it four ways.' So we summoned the courage up. The sailor had disappeared to pay the bill or go to the toilet or something like that. We sort of said, 'We're going to try to mug him.'

He'd already told us he was going to be walking up towards the railway station at the top end of the Reeperbahn, so we said we could walk him up there where there are quite shady streets and corners.

By this time, George and Paul had said, 'You want to do it, you do it. We're going back', so John and I were left. It was up to us. It was getting close to the station, so it was either a case of legging it or doing it straight away.

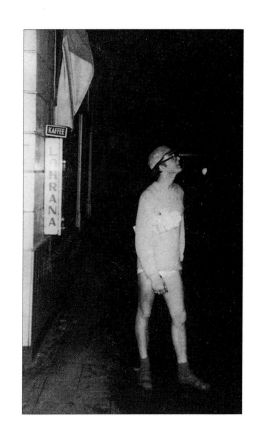

Between us, we decided it would be the next corner. There were a couple of punches thrown, and a rugby tackle to take him to the ground and grab the wallet. But he was a strong guy; sailors know how to handle themselves having been all round the world. He shrugged us off. You would if someone was trying to grab your wallet.

We got our hands on it, but the next thing, he was waving what we thought was a real gun. Many times we'd seen gas pistols and guns which were replicas; the waiters had them, people in the street had them.

But I didn't think that at the time. We just saw the gun coming and thought, 'My God, this feller's gonna blow us away!' We scattered to get away from it. We covered the first hundred yards in an Olympic record, there must have been scorch marks on the street!

We heard a blast, he was shooting at us, and we were running down the street ducking, and in the hustle and bustle we dropped the wallet. We kept on running in case this fellow chased us with the gun. We ran all the way back to the Bambi Kino, banging on the back door breathless to get in. Bang, slam the back door, didn't even look behind us.

Paul and George and Stu said, 'OK, let's whack it out', and when we breathlessly sat down and wiped the sweat off ourselves we told them what had happened. They just fell about laughing. We were saying, 'Bloody hell, we could've been killed. A stupid prank like that.' But the more we said, the more they saw the humorous side, and I suppose with them laughing at our antics, we started to see the funny side too and it ended up with all of us – in what we called the palatial suite, which was John and George's room, the one with the electric light bulb – just falling about laughing.

Then reality started to seep in once we'd started to sober up a little bit and think about it. We said, 'This guy knows who we are and where we are. My God, what if he comes back the next night and he's got his team of sailors with him? We're gonna get holes kicked out of us.'

Where before it was, 'Great English lads from Liverpool, good band', it'd be, 'Here are the bastards who tried to do you.'

So the next night we went into the Kaiserkeller very furtively. We played that night peering into the audience, dreading the fact that we might see this guy. But he never came back, much to our eternal relief. Maybe he shipped out the following morning or maybe this had happened to him before, and he just thought of it as par for the course.

But we were still very nervous. We were like that for a couple of days and it took about a week before we started to feel, 'Oh, it's over and done and dusted.'

We went to every club in the Grosse Freiheit; it was our home. We had spare time before shows, after shows, during shows. As we became more and more known, the doormen would let us in. They'd say, 'Come on, see the show.' So we saw the mud wrestling, we saw the strippers, we went to the club on the other side of the street where the telephones were.

The Grosse Freiheit was packed with clubs: the Telefon Bar where customers could phone hostesses at the tables, strip clubs, venues where girls wrestled in a pit of mud, dozens of strip joints crowded together. Side streets held other clubs, such as the Roxy Bar, popular with transsexuals and transvestites.

The Telefon Bar was quite upmarket compared with the rest of them. It was like in the films: you could see that nice-looking girl over there, and you'd phone her up to chat. But we did it with a view to having some fun.

We'd get to the state where sometimes we wouldn't phone a girl – it'd be Table Thirteen and a feller sitting there and you'd say to him, 'Love your eyes. I'm on Table Seven'. We'd laugh at it because that was our humour.

Or you'd phone some gorgeous dolly in the corner. She'd be sitting there, high class, a hostess or something and I'd go, 'Aaahhhhh!' and then stick our heads up. We'd almost always be recognised, and the minute they saw us they'd send a drink over or call us over just to have a little chat. We got away with so much in Hamburg because of who we were.

We went to the strip clubs too, and we'd be having a laugh and a joke with the strippers who'd say they would come to see our show in the evening. It was a trade-off.

Horst Fascher, who was a bouncer for Koschmider then, and a friend of ours, took us to a transvestite bar. We were told that the fellers dressed up as girls were beautiful: 'You wouldn't know the difference.' We said, 'Ah, come on, who are you kidding?' So we went in, the lot of us, walking behind Horst into the dark and murky bar. We were looking round and saying, 'No, we don't believe you, Horst. Look at them, they're gorgeous, you're winding us up.' He said, 'No I'm not, they're men.'

To counter our expressions of disbelief, he said, 'OK, go with one.' As soon as the gauntlet was thrown down, I said that John would do anything. But even John just said, 'I'll take your word for it.'

Then we started to see more of them on the street, and the usual comments would come out when they walked past, like, 'Got your bollocks strapped up, have you?' 'Had them cut off?' 'Now where did you get that pair of boobs?' Sometimes we'd be surprised because we thought they couldn't understand us, and we'd get this perfect English thrown back at us – 'Wouldn't you like to find out?'

We nearly got John involved in mud wrestling; in fact, we nearly threw him in. There was him, and I think Paul, who nearly got dumped in the mud. We'd gone in and watched the birds wrestling, throwing one another over, dumping themselves, grabbing hold of their opponents' bra straps and ripping them off and slapping them on the head with it. I said 'I wonder what would happen if John went in?' and 'There's three of us, we'll put him over the top.' But we never actually did it.

There were all sorts of weird sex gadgets in the toilets there. We used to look at them and just fall about laughing. 'Oh God, look at the size of that.' All the different things they had there: false dicks, vibrators, everything you can imagine.

On that first trip John dropped his pants on stage, and showed his arse to the audience. This was at the Kaiserkeller, which had a small rickety stage, not like playing at the Star Club, which was a converted cinema and had a high stage with curtains. But when people danced at the Kaiserkeller, they were right in your face. We were all, again, full of booze and we used to get drinks sent to us on stage. German customers would say, 'You must drink, boys, you must finish the drink', and there'd be some sessions, especially at the weekend, when the drinks were coming up faster than our playing. Then the tray of drinks would be taken away and we'd start a number and another tray'd come up: 'Prosit.'

We all decided we'd go on stage and mess about. This is when we got Paul dressing up in a sheet and me sticking something on my head, and George going on with a toilet seat round his shoulders, which we'd lifted from the toilets.

And John went on in a pair of swimming trunks. The place just erupted when we went on; but we bet John that he wouldn't show his arse to the audience. He just said, 'Watch me.' He had that little smirk on his face. We staggered on stage – to get to the Kaiserkeller stage you had to walk through the audience, with people falling about all around you.

John was in the middle of one of his numbers when he just stopped singing. He just turned round and pulled his swimming trunks down. This bare backside on stage, and he's just standing there; just for a split second there was a stunned silence, then the place erupted. This wave of sound came over and there were people banging bottles on the tables, jumping up and down.

John stayed that way for what seemed an eternity; it must have been a couple of seconds in reality. Then he pulled his swimming trunks back up again. They weren't flashy swimming trunks; they were a real scabby pair. God knows where he got them from.

Then he just continued playing. When we went back on stage again the following night, people were asking for it. They were all sitting there waiting for the big moment when John was going to drop his kecks.

There were girls who came up and said, 'Is John going to do it? Let us know when he's going to do it, we all want to be there.' But I'm sure a few of the waiters were going to pull a stunt – like throwing water on his backside.

I think John had twigged this as well, so he never did it again.

9 ▶ HOMEWARD BOUND

The Beatles' first Hamburg season came to an ignominious end. George was sent back to Liverpool for being underage, although the group intended to continue as a quartet at the Top Ten. But with the deportation of Pete and Paul, it became impossible for John and Stu to continue. So John returned home and Stuart remained with Astrid in Hamburg for several weeks more. The Hamburg experience had, however, transformed the group – and Beatlemania was about to be born on Merseyside.

Left: Pete relaxing in the garden at Hayman's Green on his return from the Beatles' first trip to Germany. They were now on the brink of conquering Liverpool.

George was sent home.

We'd had trouble with the aliens police. The myth has it that Koschmider was responsible for George's deportation, but that wasn't true. It was because we didn't have the right papers. Allan openly admits that he smuggled us into Germany because he didn't have the papers.

If we'd done four weeks of performing there, in and out, no one would have done anything. We would have been gone. But at the time we were caught, we'd been there three to four months, and it seemed that we were going to stay even longer. So the officials told us that because we were staying there and had been in the country so long, we had to go and register with the Aliens Polizei and get it cleared up. So that's when we went down to the Aliens Polizei and told them where we were working, who our employer was, how long we'd been working and all the rest.

There seemed to be no problems but we then had a situation because George was under eighteen, which conflicted with the German law at the time (the *Ausweis*). They said George could stay, but the law said that anyone under eighteen had to leave at ten o'clock at night. The *Ausweis* patrol, as we used to call it, would come in at ten o'clock and check out the kids, and if they were under eighteen they were kicked out. They said, 'George, at ten o'clock you've got to stop playing on stage.' We said, 'He can't do that. It's ridiculous. It means he's with us for half the act, then from ten o'clock until two in the morning, or whenever we finish, he's not going to be with us.' But that was the only way they would let him stay. Consequently, George said, 'It's pointless. I'm going.'

That left Stu, John, Paul and myself performing without George, and that was quite a loss. We tried to cover for him, but even though John played solo, George was the lead guitarist and his contribution to the repertoire and harmonies was radically missed.

So we were frustrated. Plus, by this time we'd had all these veiled threats from Koschmider. We were annoyed with him because we were still living in this crappy accommodation . . . and he hadn't put up a fight, we felt, to keep George. I suppose we felt he'd neglected us.

By then we'd also been round to see Tony Sheridan playing at the Top Ten. Even when George was still with us, we'd gone round as a band because we'd seen him on television and thought, 'Wow! A household name and he's only in a club round the corner!'

We suddenly realised that the Top Ten club was a far better club than Koschmider's. Better clientele, plus the sound system had echo mikes, reverbs and all that type of stuff. We were saying, 'Listen to that – he's singing with echo in his voice! It makes us look like peasants.'

We were also still after Koschmider to give us a better stage – the wooden thing bounced off beer crates. After Storm had broken it, we thought that would be the last straw and Koschmider would have to put a new stage up for us instead of this thing which, if you stamped your feet, everybody bounced up and down. All he did was part-repair the damn thing.

So we went and saw the Top Ten and there it was: stage, drum dais, carpets. Peter Eckhorn, the proprietor, recognised us and said, 'If you ever leave the Kaiserkeller come and see me. I will give you a job.'

The final straw was when we went to Koschmider to ask for more money and said, 'If you don't give us more money we're going to the Top Ten.' Koschmider said, 'If you go and play the Top Ten you'll never play in Hamburg again.'

But we said, 'You can't frighten us.' Then we went and saw Peter Eckhorn and he said, 'Fine, I'll take you on as you are and you'll play with Tony Sheridan as the house musicians.' He didn't have a house band at that time. There was also accommodation at the Top Ten on the top floor of the building. Eckhorn said, 'If you want to move your stuff in, no problem.' That meant that Paul and I had to go back to the Bambi Kino to get our stuff. Because we were living in the dungeons and there were no lights, we took some condoms and lit them and stuck them on the wall and left them sputtering. This gave us just enough light to throw our stuff into our suitcases.

The next morning, at the Top Ten, we were woken up by the German police asking for McCartney and Best. We were yanked off and didn't know what the hell was going on. We were taken to Hamburg police station. John knew we'd been taken away, but the only thing he could do was to get in touch with Stu and Astrid. By the time they found out what was going on, Paul and I had been in the police station for some time, taking quite a grilling. And even though Astrid and Stu and Eckhorn came down and asked what they could do to help, it became apparent that we were charged with attempting to burn down the Bambi Kino.

We looked at one another in astonishment, thinking, 'What's going on here?' We didn't know what was going to happen next. What did happen is that we were taken from the police station to Hamburg jail and locked up there, treated like criminals. There was a little window with a grille on it, looking down on a courtyard, where you could see convicts walking around.

We'd been driven through these big gates and we thought, 'This is the end of Paul and Pete. Locked up here with the key thrown away, and no one's going to know what's happened to us.'

The cell had two camp beds in it. We lay on them in our cowboy boots while we tried to think through what had happened and what we could do about it. Then they came in and demanded that we take our boots and socks off before we put our feet on the bed. They left us for three or four hours, then came back and said, 'You're going back to England.'

We felt relief, inasmuch as they said they'd send us back to England, but they also said, 'We're deporting you', and told us we'd be flown back in what we were standing in. So we were yanked out from the prison to the airport. I said, 'At least they're going to fly us home.'

Then we got this mad idea, while we were at the airport, to try to phone the British consul. So we did a bit of a runner, saw a telephone booth and tried to get through to the operator. We were just saying, 'Put us through to the British consul', when we were yanked out by the police. We said that we just wanted to speak to the British consul, and demanded our rights. They just ignored it, frogmarched us to the plane, stuck us on it and said, 'You're off home.'

When we came back to Liverpool we saw Allan and explained the circumstances, so Allan got us to write to the Aliens Polizei and explain it from our point of view. But instead of saying that we pinned condoms on the wall, we said we put some tapestry on the wall – to make us look like good lads, you know – 'Please take us back, it was all a mistake.' And so we said a bit of tapestry on the wall burned and smoked. The correspondence went on and the next thing we knew we were told, 'It's OK, but please make sure the next time you come to Germany you do have proper visas.'

At that time we found there was a German consul in Liverpool and all we had to do was go there and say, 'We're going to play in Germany, here's the contract', and that was it.

That was how the deportation took place, and because of it we came home in what we stood up in. Our clothes were still in Hamburg; the only thing we had were our passports, because we'd taken them with us to the police station.

My drums and Paul's guitar were still in Hamburg, too. My mother phoned Eckhorn, and he told Mo not to worry about our clothes and instruments, saying, 'I'll pack all the drums up and the guitar and the clothes and I'll send them to you.' He sent them over by ship, all crated up. I remember vividly when we got the docket saying 'Please come and collect'. We went down to one of the docks and showed the bill of lading and saw this big crate come off – and I thought, 'Ahhh! The drums and everything else are back home!'

But meanwhile, John and Stu were left in Hamburg with Sheridan. John became very disenchanted because there was no one to play with, so he decided to make his own way home. Stu said he was going to stay for the time being with Astrid. So that's how we all came back: George first, then Paul and myself, then John and eventually Stu.

Since Allan Williams didn't manage them, and with their success at getting bookings on their own, the Beatles' brief relationship with the Jacaranda clubowner ended when they returned to Liverpool. There was a certain amount of rancour because they had arranged their next German appearance directly with Peter Eckhorn for a season at the Top Ten club in Hamburg.

We didn't have much to do with Allan after that, although it was only after we came back from Germany that I got to know him a little bit better, because all of us in the group started to meet at the Jacaranda for tea and toast and coffee and marmalade. Allan would usually be there and we'd chat and he'd say, 'OK, I'll try and do that for you', but in reality, it was a case of the promoters coming to us. Once we got on the road again we were playing virtually every night.

I saw less and less of Allan. Life boiled down to doing the gig, going back home to the Casbah, and 'Where are we playing tomorrow? OK, see you there tomorrow night.' That's the way it went on.

10 ▷ LOCAL HEROES

Beatlemania was born in Liverpool. The group, now graduates of the Hamburg school of hard knocks, were to get a phenomenal reception in their home town after their initial appearance at the Casbah club on 17 December 1960.

Although they began appearing regularly at the Cavern from 1961, they also played at dozens of venues throughout Merseyside, from the Alexandria in Crosby to the Iron Door, Odd Spot – and the YMCA in Hoylake.

The direction of the Mersey scene might, however, have been very different if Allan Williams's new Liverpool club, the Top Ten, had survived. Obviously inspired by his visits to Hamburg, the Top Ten differed from other Liverpool venues, which were booked once or twice a week to present local bands. The club would instead feature resident bands seven nights a week.

The first group booked was Derry and the Seniors. This was to be followed by the Beatles on their return from Germany. But unfortunately, the club was razed to the ground in a fire, and arson was suspected.

Had the venue remained intact, the Beatles would have made their mark at a specific venue playing every night of the week. It would have become the Liverpool club most associated with the band, rather than the Cavern.

The Litherland Town Hall gig is the one that legend says was the first gig we played on coming back from Germany. It wasn't. The first one was at the Casbah.

When we came back we should have played at the Top Ten, Allan's club in Liverpool, but it burned down. That left us stranded; we had nowhere to play. So Mo said, 'You've got to have somewhere to play. I'll throw you a lifeline. I'm prepared to put you on.'

We said, 'We haven't got Stu with us', and that's when we approached Chas to cover for him.

Chas Newby, a former member of the Blackjacks, was on holiday from studying chemistry at college when the Beatles approached him to play bass guitar with them in a series of gigs, beginning with the momentous

Right: Chas Newby, former member of the Blackjacks, who played four gigs with the Beatles on their return from Hamburg in December 1960. He was temporarily replacing Stu, who had remained in Hamburg with Astrid.

Opposite: Back in Liverpool, the new-look, dynamic-sounding Beatles become a hot property at the numerous venues that made the Liverpool scene so unique.

Casbah Coffee Club show on 17 December. Chas played at four venues with them before returning to college. He claimed that John Lennon approached him asking if he was interested in going to Hamburg with the Beatles, but he turned the offer down.

At that first Casbah gig, Mo billed us as: 'the Fabulous Beatles, direct from Hamburg!'

We walked through in our leather jackets and set the equipment up, which didn't take an awful lot of time in those days. The Casbah was heaving. It was still a little mecca for rock and roll bands, and seeing this dramatic billing the buzz was out.

As we walked through, a whisper went through the club: 'Hang on, that's John, George and Paul, who used to be in the Quarry Men, and that's Pete who used to be with the Blackjacks, what's going on?'

They went to Mo and she told them, 'Rest assured, wait till they play. These are the Beatles who went to Hamburg, and this is the first gig they're playing since they returned.'

The first number we played – the impact, the leather gear, the energy, everything just hit them in the face. Then Bob Wooler, who was freelancing as a DJ and compère, got us the Litherland Town Hall gig, after much leaning on Brian Kelly.

The promoter Brian Kelly booked the Beatles for their historic Litherland Town Hall appearance on 27 December 1960 for a fee of six pounds. He was to say, 'On their first appearance I was completely knocked out by them. They had a pounding, pulsating beat which I knew would be big box office. When they had finished playing, I posted some bouncers on the door of their dressing room to prevent other promoters who were in the hall entering. I went inside and booked them solidly for months ahead.'

The first months in Hamburg were formative for the group. During that period Pete developed his noted 'atom beat', which was to influence so many other Liverpool drummers. Here he sits behind his kit on the Cavern stage.

The night of the Litherland performance the members of the Casbah disappeared. Mo said it was one of the few nights that the Casbah was empty. They all said, 'We'll have to see Pete with the Beatles', and shot off to the town hall, multiplying the normal crowd who attended Brian Kelly's dances.

We played the gig and there was this phenomenal reaction. 'The Beatles,' Bob announced, 'from Hamburg!' They were expecting us to speak German. Here we were, Liverpool lads, and people were saying 'Don't they speak English well?'

That powerful, positive reaction, the same reaction as at the Casbah, manifested itself at Litherland Town Hall, too. In fact, reaction like that had never been seen in Liverpool before. There was a crowd euphoria even before we were introduced on that particular night. Yet no one, apart from the Casbah members in the audience, knew who the Beatles were.

We were introduced and we kicked off our number. In those days, everyone used to dance. There'd be a few people at the front of the stage watching the band, and a lot of people out there dancing.

A few seconds into our first number – I think we kicked off with 'Red Sails in the Sunset' – the crowd in there stopped dancing and were physically drawn like a magnet towards the front of the stage; you had this mass of boys and girls just standing there watching the act, shouting and screaming for more.

When we came off stage, Brian Kelly came round to the changing rooms and said, 'I'll book you for Litherland Town Hall, Aintree Institute, Lathom Hall' and 'What's your price?' We said, 'Seven pounds.' He said, 'I'll pay you six pounds for some of them on a Friday and a Thursday, and seven pounds at weekends.' We said, 'That'll do.'

I had a diary. I started to take the bookings down. We were now on the Brian Kelly circuit and other bands came up and said, 'Did you get any bookings?' and I said, 'Yeah, we got so many dates at Litherland, so many dates at Aintree Institute and we're playing Lathom Hall.' And they were saying, 'God, we only get one date off him in a blue moon.'

I think Chas played four gigs with us – one at the Casbah, one at Litherland Town Hall, one at Aintree Institute and one at the Grosvenor Ballroom, Liscard. And then Stu came back, around the end of January, so we were ready to pick up the engagements.

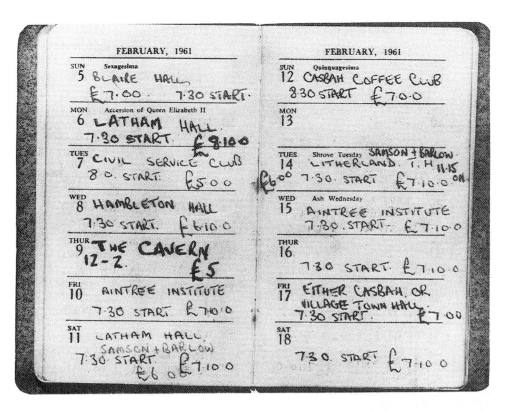

Pages from Pete's diary of February 1961 indicate how busy the group became in Liverpool on their return. An interesting aside on one of these February dates concerns Valentine's Day (also Shrove Tuesday). There were two appearances that night – at Aintree Institute and the Cassanova club at Samson and Barlow's. In 1996, a colour film emerged of the Beatles allegedly playing at the Cassanova club on the night. It is the only colour film of the Beatles featuring Pete, although it is silent and lasts less than a minute.
(Sotheby's)

Above and opposite: Two of the shots of the leather-clad Beatles at the Cavern, commissioned for the new local publication, *Mersey Beat*. The media in those times did not consider local groups good copy, and radio and TV were still only available to chart acts. So the only regular publicity the Beatles received was in *Mersey Beat*, which remains an accurate chronicle of their early growth.

Mo had seen other promoters booking dancehalls, so she said, 'Fine, don't see why we shouldn't', and that's why she started at St John's in Tuebrook, and at Knotty Ash Village Hall. She started doing them on a regular basis; she had the ace pulling card: she put the Beatles on. A lot of people have said she tried to take over the band, but she was never interested in managing us.

As regards handling the band at the time, I was mainly responsible for it – talking to promoters and dealing with them. People got in touch, thinking, 'We'll talk to Pete 'cause he's handling the booking side of it.' It was not management, it was just making the deals and taking the bookings – and we'd make sure the equipment got to such and such a place.

Mo was amazed by our popularity. She said, 'I haven't seen this response before.

It's happening in Liverpool, it happened in Germany, why can't we let other people know about it?' And as television is the biggest medium, she said, 'If no one else will do it, I'll try and do it.' So she wrote to some producer at Granada. She said 'There's this great band, the Beatles, happening in Liverpool. It'll be in your interest to look at them and get them on television.'

Mo was just so impressed with the band. OK, I was part of it, so I suppose, as with everything else I did, she was interested in it on my account. But it was because she believed in us as a group. She wasn't pushing me, she was pushing the Beatles.

The myth that a beating in Liverpool led to Stuart Sutcliffe's eventual death first saw light in the book by Allan Williams and William Marshall, *The Man Who Gave The Beatles Away*. In it, Allan claimed that Stuart was attacked outside Litherland Town Hall, and kicked in the head by a local thug. There is no evidence that such an event took place.

But the Lathom Hall incident happened. Of the four people involved, John and Stu are dead, but Pete Best and Neil Aspinall, a driver for the band, both remember the fight. Neil described it in a 1966 interview in *Rave*, when he said, 'At Lathom Hall two troublemakers followed Stu Sutcliffe into the dressing room muttering things like "Get your hair cut, girl!" John and Pete saw this and went after them. A fight broke out and John broke his little finger. It set crooked and never straightened.'

As to what caused Stu's haemorrhage, his mother, Millie, always maintained that it was the result of a fall down the steps of his attic studio in Astrid's house outside Hamburg.

When Stu came back there was an incident at Lathom Hall. Lathom was reputed to be a tough gig. While we were on stage there was a gang of lads who picked on Stu.

When we'd done our session and come off, we changed, which didn't take an awful lot of time because we basically played in what we stood up in. Stu went out, followed by John and myself.

These lads started a fight with Stu after picking on him. We got to know about it because some people ran back to the side of the stage where we had to come from and said, 'Stu's getting the living daylights knocked out of him.'

So John and I dashed out. We threw a couple of punches, sorted things out and pulled Stu back in again. Then we turned to the lads and said, 'What the hell's going on? What the hell are you picking on him for? He hasn't done anything. We're only here to do a job, we're playing; so go away and behave yourselves.' And it was left at that.

The fact that John and I had pitched in and got involved made these lads feel a certain amount of respect for us. It was a case of 'No, they're OK, they're good lads, leave them alone.' We didn't have to fear Lathom Hall at all after that. When we played there again they were all saying, 'All right, lads!' We were now one of the boys.

As a result of the fight John broke a little finger. He still managed to play for a couple of gigs after that. He hadn't complained or said, 'I broke my finger', it was just 'That's hurting a bit.' The next time we saw him he had a splint on it.

When people talk of Stu being beaten up, I think it stems from this incident. But I don't remember Stu getting to the stage where he had his head kicked in, as some legends say, alleging that this caused his fatal brain haemorrhage.

For as long as I was with the band I can only remember two incidents when fists were thrown and Stu was involved. The Lathom Hall incident aside, the other occasion was at the Top Ten Club, and that was between Paul and Stu. Paul took the mick out of Astrid and Stu lost his temper and took a swing at him.

Meanwhile, the membership of the Casbah continued to grow, and Mo said, 'OK, just in case there's any trouble, I'll get a doorman' – in other words, a bouncer. It was a deterrent more than anything else. So she advertised, and Frank Garner and another guy called Norman saw Mo. Frank said, 'I'm a black belt in judo and Norman's a brown belt.'

I was having some problems getting all the stuff to the gigs. It wasn't too bad for the other lads because they jumped on the bus, but it still meant the drums and amplifiers had to be taken to the venue, and we were hiring taxis for the purpose, or lugging it all on a bus. It was rough.

Frank saw us going through all this and said, 'Look, give me a quid for petrol and I'll run you to the gigs, I'll drop the stuff off there. You tell me what time you finish, I'll be there, load the van and take you back. Simple.'

He also said, 'If any of the lads need a lift, they can squeeze in the back, and I'll bring them back to the Casbah.' That's why, on many nights, John stayed at the Casbah. We got dropped off there and the club would be closed by the time we got back so we'd go downstairs and load ourselves up with Coke and crisps and play records until two or three in the morning.

Frank was our first driver. And everything seemed OK, but it reached a point where there were certain nights Frank couldn't do it. He'd say, 'No, I've got judo classes.' Sometimes he'd take turns with Norman.

That's when Neil Aspinall took over. Neil had become friends with the family and we said, 'Get yourself a little van, do the driving. We'll pay you a quid a night, you run us round, same thing, drop us off. Stay there if you want, or come back and pick us up.' So Neil started doing that, while he was still working as a trainee accountant.

We'd first got to know Neil through the Casbah. He just came down to the club as a member. Neil's first van was a battered old wreck, maroon and grey. But it solved the difficulty we were in as it went from A to B, and it took the equipment. The problem was, you couldn't lock it.

When it was a case of dropping the equipment off, if it was a lunchtime session, instead of saying, 'I'll come back and pick you up', Neil would say, 'What's the point? I'll take you down, by the time I get back home I've gotta come back again.' So he said, 'I'll sit here.'

At times like that we brought in the family dog, a big bull mastiff called Satan,

Cavern owner Ray McFall. He was to book the Beatles for 292 Cavern sessions. The advice of his DJ Bob Wooler proved invaluable and with the success of the Beatles and other Mersey groups, the club was to become internationally famous.

The Beatles make the Cavern club their home. Although they were now to make regular appearances at the venue, they continued to play in other jive hives around the city. (Apple Corps)

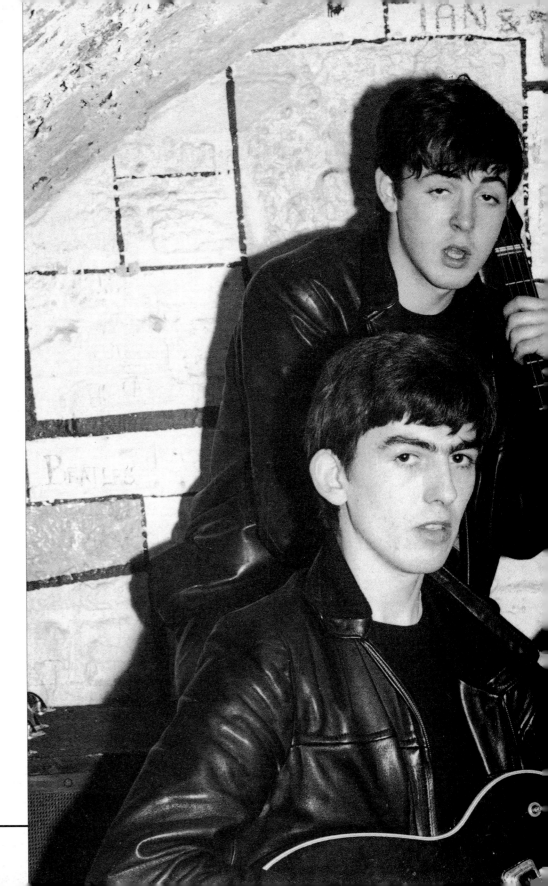

THE BEST YEARS
OF THE BEATLES

a massive feller. We'd load Satan into the van, and he was our watchdog. We'd unload all the equipment and leave Satan in the back of the van. There were no locks, but if anyone bumped or hammered against the van, a massive bull mastiff would appear – Grrrrrr! His head used to fill the window. It was enough to frighten anyone. Just one look at it, and they'd disappear down the road.

That van got us around. Neil kept it, doctored it, got it fixed up and running, kept doing repairs to it, until Epstein took over the management and he bought the Beatles a better van.

We made our Cavern debut at a lunchtime session. This is something that Bob Wooler said he was instrumental in getting for us. He said he put pressure on Ray McFall, the Cavern's manager, to get us to play there. But I know that Mo also spoke to Ray McFall about booking us. I'm not saying it wasn't Bob – it could have been a combination of Bob putting pressure on him and Mo phoning at the same time.

When we first heard there were lunchtime sessions at the Cavern we went down there. The first show we went to before we actually played there was Johnny Hutch, playing with the Big Three. He knew who we were, so he said, 'Hi, how're you doing?' and we said, 'We're going to play a lunchtime

Pete, George, John and Paul, in the Cavern bandroom, waiting to perform before the troglodytes. (Michael McCartney)

session.' Word got out, and the first lunchtime session we played the crowd was a lot bigger than it normally was. Because of that, Ray McFall booked us again. The next time we played word had spread, and the place was heaving.

As a result of these early lunchtime sessions, he started to give us evening work, mixing the permutations, putting the Beatles on with a jazz band until the Cavern went over to a complete rock sound.

The Cavern had initially shunned rock and roll. From its opening in 1957 it was primarily a jazz club which deigned to book the occasional skiffle group. The Quarry Men, in their first (skiffle) incarnation, had appeared there only once, on 7 August 1957. On that occasion, John Lennon attempted to sing some Elvis Presley songs. Owner Alan Sytner sent a note to him on stage, saying, 'Cut out the bloody rock!'

Even when Ray McFall took over the club, rock and roll was anathema. When Rory Storm and the Hurricanes sang 'Whole Lotta Shakin'', they were pelted with coins by the jazz fans and McFall fined them.

The Cavern didn't relax its attitudes towards rock until 1961. The Beatles made their debut there in February of that year.

Waning jazz audiences and the growth of rock and roll around the city inspired Ray McFall to begin booking rock groups. It should be acknowledged, however, that by the time the Cavern became interested, other pioneering promoters had created a thriving scene. There were almost 400 different bands and artists who had played and developed their music in venues around the city – including, of course, the Beatles, who had learned their craft at the Casbah Club.

We had a spell at the Cavern, but we were still doing a couple of Casbah gigs and a couple of Mo's promotions. Then more and more work came in from the Cavern, and it tended to become our regular venue. Ray McFall was booking us along with a lot of other bands. So we'd take it in turns – Gerry and the Pacemakers, Rory Storm, the Big Three, the Searchers, Faron, the Remo Four and everyone else who was around.

Then there was the Iron Door, and we used to play there. Whoever booked us we played for. We didn't really have an allegiance to anyone: 'You give us your money, we'll play your venue', it was as simple as that.

A popular piece of Beatle lore is that Brian Epstein discovered the Beatles when a boy walked into Nems (North End Music Stores, a chain run by Brian's family) on 28 October 1961 to ask for a record they'd made in Hamburg. Brian opened his book, *A Cellarful of Noise*, with this tale. In fact, Brian became very interested in the Beatles when he first read about them in *Mersey Beat* in July 1961. He became a record reviewer with the third issue, and was always asking for more information about the Beatles than appeared in stories in the paper. He learned about their record in issue No. 2 of *Mersey Beat*, published on 20 July 1961, and was acutely aware of their visits to his store prior to their second visit to Hamburg at the end of March in 1961.

We began going to Nems more often once we'd started doing the Cavern lunchtime sessions. The usual thing was to get to the club around half past eleven. Neil and I would go there in the van and get there at eleven o'clock to carry the stuff down. The lads themselves stuck them on stage after throwing my drums on stage. Then we'd wait for the place to open. We usually played from half past twelve to one and from half past one to two.

We'd relax a little bit after the show, then would wander over to the Grapes and have a couple of pints in there. The Grapes closed at three o'clock and soon after we'd wander over to Nems. The girls would know us as soon as we walked in: 'Here they are.'

Normally we all went there together and used to do the same thing every time: come in, walk over to the record counter, look at the list of new releases and listen to them. We'd make our decision about a number there and then.

We'd listen to both sides of a record, not just the 'A' side, in the listening booths there. It was a case of just listening, and then someone would say, 'I'm gonna do that', and that number would be theirs. John was like that with 'Boys', or George would have picked Joe Brown and the Bruvvers with 'Picture of You'.

What we would do was get them to play it two or three times. We'd scribble the words down, or the chord sequence. 'I'd love to get that record. I'll get it,' someone would say. We'd write the words down, come back and rehearse it a couple of times. We'd often try it at the Cavern after we'd finished playing. We did a bit of rehearsing, but it wasn't all that much in those days. We'd say, 'Yeah, it's good enough, we'll do it tonight', and we'd polish it up as we performed it on stage in front of the audience.

When we were at Nems we were very conscious of Brian, because whenever we went there there always used to be this guy who would flutter down the stairs, cast a furtive glance over to us, a look of disbelief – 'Oh, it's *them* again.' Then he'd disappear again up the stairs.

Afterwards, he laughed and joked about it, saying, 'Whenever you came into the shop the word was out. As far as selling records was concerned downstairs, it just came to a standstill, you know, because all the girls were too interested in helping the Beatles or talking to the Beatles while you were there.'

He said it wasn't too bad once a week, but there'd be times when we'd go in three or four times a week!

THE BEST YEARS
OF THE BEATLES

11 ▷ IN MY LIVERPOOL HOME

Pete's father, Johnny Best, had spent the Second World War on a posting to India, where he worked as a physical training instructor. He met his future wife, Mona – who was working for the Red Cross at the time – in Delhi. They were eventually married there. Their first son, Randolph Peter Best, was born on 24 November 1941. His brother Rory was born in 1944, also in India.

Although I regard Liverpool as my home, I was born in India. My mother's side of the family were English people who went over to India during the Raj.

She got to know my father during the war. She was working for the Red Cross. My dad, Johnny Best, was born and bred in Liverpool. He later became a boxing promoter and a lot of people recognise his name from that. But during the war he had signed up with the Army and the Navy and was a PE teacher.

Well respected, he trained ghurkas and commandos. After he'd been shipped over there he met and fell in love with Mo, and that was it. I was born over there, my middle brother Rory was born out there, so I suppose you could say we are war babies, from India. In Bombay, where we lived, we overlooked Bombay beach, so a lot of times we'd be taken down to play on the beach. When Dad finished his service over there and was coming back to England, Mo came back with him. We sailed on the troopship *Georgic* in December 1945. Things which stick in my mind about the *Georgic* are that Rory learned to walk on it, we went through force ten gales – and I learned to swear.

I used to go with Rory through the closed walkways so there wouldn't be any danger of being swept overboard. I was the elder brother and he was still wobbling about, with me holding on to him as the ship lurched backwards and forwards. The troops asked Mo if they could take the kids down to their quarters to entertain them.

Left: Johnny Best with Rory and Pete. Johnny had been a noted Liverpool boxing promoter who had staged fights with boxers such as Randolph Turpin and Floyd Patterson shortly before the war.

Right: Pete, aged one year and nine months. He was born in Madras on 24 November 1941.

Far right: Pete holds younger brother Rory in his arms on the verandah of their home in Bombay in April 1945.

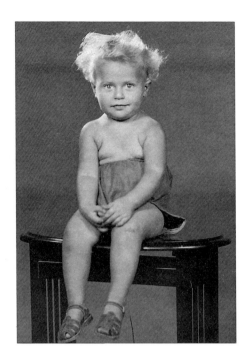

I suppose we were adopted by them, and they found it amusing to have a four-year-old kid coming out with a mouthful, not knowing what it was. They'd say, 'Go back and tell your dad that we said this' – and it was eff this, the biggest load of swear words you could think of. And I toddled back, or they'd take me back, and Mo and Dad would be saying, 'Where did you pick that up from?'

Mo would have a good banter with the troops when she saw them, saying, 'You're giving Pete a good education. Even though he doesn't realise it, by the time we get back to Liverpool and we dock he's going to be able to swear twice as well as you lot.'

I've never been back. That is one of the things I'd like to see on my travels now. I'll either get back to see it because we're touring out there, or, if it doesn't happen that way, I must go back and see which things I can still remember.

The Best family arrived back in Liverpool in 1945, and lived in a flat on Casey Street for two years before finally settling in at the house at 8 Hayman's Green, West Derby. Pete eventually won a scholarship to Liverpool Collegiate, one of Liverpool's premier grammar schools, where he achieved five 'O' levels. He first took an interest in performing music at the age of sixteen. Pete and Rory's younger brother Roag was born in Liverpool.

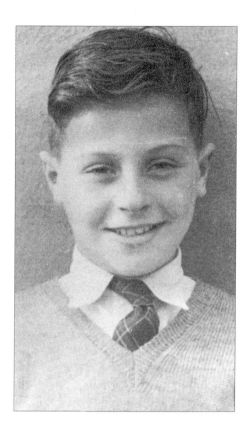

When we arrived in Liverpool, I didn't know anything at all about it. I had never been out of India. At that age I wasn't upset at leaving home, but Mo was upset, as she was leaving her parents – years afterwards, my grandparents came over to England and lived with Mum, so we saw an awful lot more of them in the later years.

The thing that was really different was the weather. I remember it was cold when we disembarked, and that's something we'd never experienced in India. I remember Mo putting her coat on and buttoning it up. Normally, in India, I'd tag along with a pair of baggy shorts on, chukka sandals, sometimes I wouldn't even put a shirt on.

But kids adapt to things very quickly. I think the ones who were worrying about what was going to happen next, picking up the pieces, were Dad and Mo.

When we first came home we lived at what used to be the Best household, at Ellersley, a big detached house in its own grounds with large gardens where Dad's family lived. From a kid's point of view it was fine, this big lawn to play on with Rory.

Antrag

auf Erteilung eines Sichtvermerks zur Einreise nach — zur Durchreise durch — Deutschland

Application for a Visa to enter — to travel through — Germany

Demande de délivrance d'un visa d'entrée en — de transit par — l'Allemagne

An d.___ Botschaft— Gesandtschaft	— Generalkonsulat der Bundesrepublik Deutschland
To the Embassy— Legation	— Consulate-General of the Federal Republic of Germany
Ambassade— Légation	— Consulat Général de la République fédérale d'Allemagne

in/in/à ENGLAND (LIVERPOOL)

1. Familien- und Vornamen (bel Frauen auch Geburtsname) 1. Surname and Christian names (in the case of married women state also maiden name) 1. Nom de famille et prénoms (pour les femmes, nom de jeune fille)	BEST (Familienname) (Surname) (Nom de famille) RANDOLPH PETER (Vornamen, Rufname unterstreichen) (Christian names, underline name by which usually known) (prénoms, souligner le prénom usuel)
2. Geburtstag und Geburtsort (Kreis, Land) 2. Date and place of birth (county, country) 2. Date et lieu de naissance (département, pays)	geboren am 24 NOV. 1941 Born on né le in MADRAS INDIA in à (Kreis Land) (county country) (département pays)
3. Wohnsitz oder dauernder Aufenthaltsort, Sitz der gewerblichen Niederlassung, ge- naue Anschrift und Geschäftsadresse 3. Domicile or permanent residence, and seat of business establishment, exact private and business address 3. Domicile ou lieu de résidence perma- nente, siège de l'entreprise, adresse exacte privée et commerciale	136 KIEPERBAHN TOP TEN CLUB HAMBURG ALTONA HAMBURG GERMANY
4. Familienstand 4. Marital Status 4. Situation de famille	ledig SINGLE Single célibataire verheiratet, verwitwet, geschieden seit .... Married, widowed, divorced since .... marié, veuf, divorcé depuis ....
5. Staatsangehörigkeit (bei Doppelstaatern auch die weitere) 5. Nationality (in case of dual nationality state second nationality) 5. Nationalité (en cas de double nationalité, indiquer aussi la seconde)	jetzige BRITISH SUBJECT Present nationality actuelle frühere Former nationality d'origine zweite Staatsangehörigkeit Second nationality seconde nationalité
6. Beruf 6. Trade or profession 6. Profession	MUSICIAN

Kons. 11
50000 · 9·60· Gebr. Medinger Bonn

12 ▶ THE TOP TEN

Peter Eckhorn was given the premises of 136 Reeperbahn by his father when he was only twenty-one. It had formerly been called the Hippodrome and was home to a topless circus. Eckhorn decided to turn it into a rock and roll club, and renamed it the Top Ten. Copying the pattern of the Kaiserkeller, he hired Horst Fascher, former bouncer of that club, and also booked Tony Sheridan after he'd left Koschmider's club. The Beatles appeared at the Top Ten from 27 March until 2 July 1961 – a total of nearly 100 nights.

Unlike Liverpool, where there were numerous rock clubs, Hamburg seemed only able to support one or two at a time. The competition from the Top Ten caused Koschmider to turn the Kaiserkeller back into a strip club. And once the Star Club opened, the Top Ten began to wane.

We'd made the approach to Peter Eckhorn, who managed the Top Ten club in Hamburg, and he said, 'Look, if you want to come back to Germany, let me know.' So we decided to give it another crack – plus, Stu was interested in going back because of Astrid.

I phoned Eckhorn and he gave me some dates. I said I'd have to check it with the others. They were showing interest, but I never knew what their reaction would be. I might say, 'I've got you two months in Hamburg', and they could give me a raspberry and say, 'On your bike!'

But the money was good and when I mentioned that to the other lads they said, 'Yeah, fine.' So I contacted Eckhorn again and booked in the dates. Among ourselves, because of what had happened before, we decided we'd better do things properly this time, and we went to the German consul to get our passports stamped. Then we made our way over. We went by train this time, and it was quite a lengthy trip.

Tony Sheridan, then house musician at the Hamburg Top Ten, is a legendary figure in the Beatles story. A musician born in Cheltenham in 1940, he'd appeared on TV shows such as *Oh Boy* and *Boy Meets Girl* before he joined the first band to appear at the Kaiserkeller – the Jets. When the Jets disbanded he remained in Hamburg. Despite his undoubted talent, he never achieved major success outside of Germany.

Left: **Pete's application form to obtain a visa to work at the Top Ten in Hamburg. On their previous trip to Hamburg they'd been smuggled in on the pretext that they were students.**

Above and opposite: **Two shots of the Beatles on stage at the Top Ten. Paul is shown playing piano. It was decided that as they backed Tony Sheridan, it would be better to have Paul on piano rather than have five guitarists.**
(K&K Studios/Redferns)

Tony Sheridan was still very much the house musician. We thought we'd have our own show and then back him, but in fact Tony played every set that we played. So we played our numbers and he played his numbers. He liked us backing him because, again, there was this harmony, the great harmonies we used to do for him.

So with the numbers that he performed, he'd have three people harmonising with him, which produced a great overall sound. As he was such a versatile guitarist, it was good for him to work on our numbers because there could be times when George would say, 'This is the way to do the song', and I think George learned one or two things from Sheridan as well. It was a good education.

People are wrong if they say that John copied his stance on stage from Sheridan. John had that stance before, even from the early days when I remember him. He always tended to have that little crouch. Sheridan always held his guitar quite high, but he wasn't as bent over as John. There was a certain stoop to the mike which everyone does when they're performing, but John had more of a squat down in front of the mike.

We had crowded houses every night. We'd start off the set when the club first opened at seven. The audience for the first set would be quite small, as people were just starting to come in, but towards the middle of the evening you were always guaranteed that the place was full. At weekends, Friday, Saturday and Sunday, there was standing room only. The club would be full at seven o'clock, with people queuing to get in and it would stay like that till one o'clock in the morning.

We played as many hours as we had done at the Kaiserkeller. I think the breaks we had were a little bit longer, but we were still doing six or seven hours a night. This schedule had proved of great benefit when we went back to Liverpool that first time. After doing all those hours every night, when promoters asked us to play for an hour – what a breeze!

We went to Hamburg the second time realising that we were going back to this six or seven hours a night slog, but the money was good and we thought, 'There are other things that compensate for the long hours when we're over there.' We'd be playing with Sheridan, and it was a great club. We'd seen it before and we'd have a chance to play it properly with Sheridan and take full advantage of the echo mikes.

By the time we went back it was, in fact, the top club in Hamburg. The Kaiserkeller was still there, but it was suffering. Very much so. Once word got out that we were back in Hamburg again, playing the Top Ten in the Reeperbahn, it was like another stab wound to Koschmider: his figures fell. But it was great for Peter Eckhorn.

It was Peter who tipped us off that Bert Kaempfert was in the audience. He'd recognised Kaempfert, noticed he was watching the band, seemed interested and had come back again to have another look, another listen.

Berthold Kaempfert was a prominent figure in the German show business world, with an American number one hit, 'Wonderland by Night'. In 1961 he was voted 'Bandleader of the Year' in *Cashbox* and went on to pen further hits such as 'A Swinging Safari', 'Strangers in the Night' and 'Spanish Eyes'. He died of a heart attack in 1980.

Kaempfert started to come quite regularly; he began to request certain songs, such as 'My Bonnie', 'The Saints' and 'Take Out Some Insurance' – also known as 'If You Love Me Baby' – the tracks he was later to record. Then he approached us and said 'I want to record you.' Of course, everyone was totally over the moon. We didn't know who Kaempfert was initially, but Eckhorn and other people said, 'Bert Kaempfert – he's a legend in Germany. Top A&R man, record producer, a household name in Germany.'

So we said, 'Now he wants to record us. Where's the paper? Sign!' We didn't even think about it until afterwards. We were just paid a session fee. It's been alleged that we opted for a session fee rather than royalties because we didn't like the recordings, but that's untrue.

Kaempfert wanted the contract signed before we went to the school hall to record, and it was presented as: 'That is the deal you're going to get.' He said he'd pay us a certain amount and I think at the time we just thought, 'What the hell, we're recording! We could have a number one in Germany!' We were very naive.

We had a dilemma with the recording because by this time there had been that little bit of fisticuffs between Paul and Stu.

When Kaempfert wanted to record us, we were faced with the same problem – having four guitarists. Paul was playing piano at the Top Ten and Stu was still playing bass, simply because Sheridan was playing guitar with us.

Since this was our first real recording opportunity, there'd been talk among ourselves about letting Paul play bass on the sessions. It wasn't a case of 'Paul's gotta play bass, so Stu, you're out!' We'd heard Paul play bass on 'Love Me Tender', so we were wondering how to tell Stu we wanted Paul to do it on the recording.

But we didn't have to make that decision, because it was around that time that Stu came up and said 'I'm leaving the band.' So the fact that he left the band and went to the State College of Art in Hamburg and stayed with Astrid meant that Paul stepped in as bass player.

Paul hadn't shown any leanings towards it. I mean, when we went back to Hamburg and had Sheridan join us, Paul realised there would be too many guitarists and was quite prepared to play piano. If Stu wanted to go off stage for a couple of minutes, or sing a song, then Paul would quite happily take Stu's place and play the bass upside down, or whatever you have to do if you're left-handed.

Stu seemed quite happy to be in the band: his performance on stage never went down. There was some turmoil in his mind, which must have been to do with his decision to leave the band for Astrid and art college, because he thought so much about the Beatles and being a Beatle. But he kept his feelings to himself.

The fight between Stu and Paul had been coming for quite some time because Stu, as I've said, would look at Astrid when she was in the audience and play to her. He was madly in love with the girl, so what was wrong with that? He took some gentle banter from us, but Paul kept winding him up. On this particular night Astrid was there and Paul said something. I don't actually know what the remark was because Paul was playing piano on the other side of the drum rostrum. Stu took his bass off and it wasn't with a view to giving it to anyone. He put it down and the next thing, the two of them were swinging at one another.

When it happened, the audience seemed bewildered, obviously thinking, 'Hang on, this isn't "*mach shau*", this is really happening.' Astrid was horrified. It was quickly stopped. George, John and I dashed over. There were a few more words from them, such as 'We'll finish it later', and that type of stuff. We said, 'No, you won't finish it, it's over and done with now. You go back and play the piano and you put your bass back on and we'll start the show.' We told them not to be silly.

It never happened again. Stu left not long after that. Even so, I don't think that incident accelerated his departure. Stu was already wondering how he was going to tell the boys he was going to leave the band. I don't think Stu was one to carry grudges. We had an inkling of his decision to leave before he told us. It didn't come as a tremendous shock to us.

The repertoire at the Top Ten included numbers like 'Beautiful Dreamer' and 'Over the Rainbow'. When it came to recording, 'My Bonnie' and 'The Saints' were Kaempfert's choices, not ours.

We'd played them on stage because the German audiences loved 'The Saints'. Then Sheridan did 'My Bonnie', because it was also a popular song in German and again we played around with the arrangement and came out with the slow intro, a bit Presleyish, then it turned into an out-and-out raving rocker, which the German audiences loved.

But Kaempfert picked up on it because he was looking at what was going to sell to German audiences. He'd seen the response to these particular numbers which the Beatles did. 'Ain't She Sweet' was another number which the German audiences would respond to – and 'Cry For a Shadow' simply because it was so different.

I'm still fascinated by the sound of 'Cry For a Shadow'. Some said, 'What! The Beatles playing an instrumental!' But it went down well. So I think credit must go to Kaempfert.

He'd come in, he'd watched, he'd seen which numbers had gone down with the crowds. They were good arrangements, the harmonies were in there, they were powerful, even explosive. And these were the numbers we recorded.

The Beatles backed Tony Sheridan during recording sessions on a mobile recording unit at the infants' school, Harburg Friedrich Ebert Halle, in May 1961. The Beatles were not credited under their own name, but were referred to as the Beat Brothers. Since Sheridan recorded a number of tracks with different personnel he credited as the Beat Brothers, some tracks have been wrongly credited to the Beatles. During the three-day session they completed the numbers 'The Saints', 'Why', 'My Bonnie', 'Ain't She Sweet', 'Cry For a Shadow' and possibly 'If You Love Me Baby' and 'Nobody's Child'.

Although some of the songs were 'oldies', they were genuinely appropriate in a rock repertoire. 'My Bonnie', written in 1881, had been recorded as a rock number by Ray Charles in August 1958. 'The Saints', another traditional tune more commonly known as 'The Saints Go Marching In', had also been recorded as a rock and roll number by Bill Haley and the Comets in March 1956. The Beatles would have heard both versions and would have played similar arrangements.

'Ain't She Sweet', penned in 1927, was also given the rock treatment by Gene Vincent in a version released on his *Bluejean Bop* album in August 1956. This was the only track of the sessions to feature a Beatle on lead vocals when John sang the number.

'If You Love Me Baby' was originally recorded by Jimmy Reed in 1959.

'Cry For a Shadow' was an instrumental composed by George Harrison in response to a challenge from Rory Storm to parody the Shadows. It was the only original Beatles number recorded by Kaempfert.

A front cover story detailing the sessions, under the heading 'Beatles Sign Recording Contract!', was featured in Issue No. 2 of *Mersey Beat*, published on 20 July 1961. Brian Epstein saw this issue and was intrigued by the fact that a local group had made a record.

We socialised with Sheridan a lot. We were practically living in each others' pockets. In the same quarters upstairs at the Top Ten, playing on stage together; even after the show, we'd go and eat at the same place and then, once we'd finished there, we'd usually climb back up the stairs to the attic again. If we were rehearsing a number, Tony'd come down and he'd sit in and say, 'I may as well get to know it, as I'm going to be playing it with you.'

Initially we were a bit awestruck by Tony. Then, because of playing with him, living together, doing the same things together, we developed as friends and comrades.

When we went back to Germany for the second time, Sheridan was playing at the Star Club, so we tended to do the same things again, go off to get a beer, knock around with each other.

But I've had my moments with Tony. I've had a fight with him, in fact. It was just one of those things. He picked on me on a night when I wasn't going to take any of it, and I said, 'Sod off! This is it.' We slugged it out in the hallway, battered hell out of one another, but there was mutual respect after that. At the end of it we were still friends. We shook hands and called it a day.

As far as the group's musical progress was concerned, once the improvement had started it didn't stop. It wasn't like we reached a plateau. When we went back to Hamburg the reaction was 'They are back, and they're even better.' When we returned to Liverpool it was the same. It was like a growing experience; the music was improving all the time, it was becoming stronger.

I still say the long hours helped, despite people saying you can get stale playing long hours. You can, but I think when you're playing to a live audience there is a difference. The adrenaline flows, the reaction from the audience always takes you to another level. That's what the act is all about: feeling the warmth from the audience.

The Beatles Fan Club presents **An Evening with John, George, Paul & Pete**

At The Cavern 7-30 pm Thursday 5th April 1962

Tickets 6s 6d

Purchasers of tickets will receive a FREE photograph, and may apply for free membership of the Fan Club

Guest Artists will include **The Four Jays** and the Beatles' favourite Compere **Bob Wooler**

the Beatles for their fans

Photo: Marrion   Layout: Swerdlow

Tickets available from NEMS Whitechapel or Gt Charlotte St and at The Cavern Club

Printed by Swale (Widnes) Ltd

An advertisement from *Mersey Beat* for the Beatles special fan club night at the Cavern. (The design, utilising an Albert Marrion photograph, was by Alan Swerdlow, a former pupil of Liverpool College of Art.)

13 ▷ THE FANS

The official Beatles fan club, formed in May 1962, was originally run by Bobbie Brown. During that time there was a hard core of female fans, particularly at Cavern sessions, who were devoted followers of the Beatles. Margaret Carrington was a Cavern regular and says, 'Pete Best's name was the one the girls all whispered in the dark.'

The first inkling that we had a fan club was when we came back to Liverpool from the Top Ten. This is before Brian became involved with us, so I'm talking about a period from June to October 1961.

We had a fan club night at the David Lewis Club. There wasn't an official fan club, but fans had asked if they could set one up, and we said OK. But there were a lot of problems on that particular night, and the sound system failed. I think, though, that a seed was planted that was later to grow into the official fan club.

That night I did my party piece. I used to do a couple of numbers, 'Matchbox' and 'Peppermint Twist'. It was the Joey Dee number 'Peppermint Twist' I performed, not the Paul McCartney composition 'Pinwheel Twist', which some people have wrongly attributed to the occasion. I used to let Paul get on the drums and I'd come down to the front and dance the twist. While I was singing, something happened to the sound: the amps went off. It meant that there weren't any instruments, so it was my turn to improvise. I started messing about with the Presley number 'Rose Goes Wild in the Country', and started leaping off stage and running down and sitting on the girls' laps, pretending to do a Presley.

There were some people there who were disappointed because we couldn't perform due to the sound failure, but fans enjoyed it because there was a lot of spontaneous wit and it became more like a party night.

There was also an official night at the Cavern. This was the one after Epstein had signed us, and I remember the place was heaving to capacity.

I did 'Peppermint Twist', with Paul on drums. I came to the front and danced the twist with Kathy, my future wife. She was a Kingtwister then, a dancer at gigs. I remember that out of the blue I yanked her up, pulled her through the bandroom and got her on stage. We did the twist, and Paul came back off drums and I began to play them again. It was good, and again it was a case of everyone being there to enjoy themselves.

Among the fans were the diehard regulars, the ones who were always first in the queue and in the front row. They'd tap us on the shoulder and say 'How're you doing?' You were aware that there were other fans out there, but there were some who were more forthcoming or more outgoing, and made themselves known to you.

Kathy was a fan of the music, but as to being a fan of the members of the band, she'd always said she wasn't. She had other favourites, and she said she got the impression from us that we were bigheads. Kathy was always at the dances. She'd go from the Orrell Park Ballroom to the Aintree Institute to the Cavern. She really wanted to dance.

She'd say, 'Where are we going tonight?' and her friend Alice would say, 'I want to go and see the Beatles' and Kathy would say, 'No, I want to go and see someone else.' So they'd come to a compromise and it'd be 'OK, we'll go and see the Beatles three times this week and see some other bands twice.' Kathy liked the beat, she liked the excitement, but she wanted to see other bands too.

And there were so many other bands in Liverpool. These days many seem to think that it was the Beatles and no one else. Far from it.

The effect of the rivalry between groups has been overlooked. We were all friends, and we knew where to find each other. There was this mass of musicians who at any given point during the day you could find at the places they'd frequent. If you wanted to see somebody you didn't really have to make an appointment, you'd just go and find them.

A friendly rivalry developed and it was that that was making people strive to achieve things. It was improving the music. Groups were competing to be the first to perform certain numbers. Our source was going down to Nems and listening to the new releases when they came out. You had other bands who'd say, 'The Beatles haven't done this number, so we'll do it.'

'Some Other Guy' – that became the Big Three's song. The same with 'Mashed Potatoes' and the Undertakers. The Beatles would never dream of playing 'Mashed Potatoes', it was the Undertakers' number – fine. There were certain numbers which we'd listen to and just say 'No' to. And there'd be other bands who, because we'd said 'No' to it, would put it into their repertoire.

If you were a fan, it was great, because they had all these bands contending with each other to be the first to do a number or to bring new material into the act.

The unsung heroes were the promoters. They were prepared to help the scene to grow, utilising places and venues – everything from church halls, dance halls, swimming baths, coffee bars and women's institutes to YMCAs. They were saying, 'I'll put on a band if I have a stage – or even if I don't have a stage.'

By this time the number of venues on Merseyside was staggering. There were over 350 social clubs affiliated to the Merseyside Clubs Association, and scores of other venues promoting local groups – from the Silver Blades Ice Rink and the New Brighton Baths (which held Beat and Bathe dances), to ballrooms, town halls, synagogues, cellar clubs and coffee bars.

This vast number of venues was one of the reasons why so many groups proliferated on Merseyside: there were over 400 different bands in existence during the heyday of Mersey Beat.

It was great. The Orrell Park Ballroom, with Ralph Webster, was no more than a stone's throw from the Aintree Institute, which was Brian Kelly's. On the same night you'd have Ralph with the Undertakers at the Orrell Park Ballroom, and Brian Kelly with the Beatles at Aintree Institute – and both places would be jumping. Talking to Ralph, he said, 'Yeah, people didn't realise it was a case of there being an understanding between Brian and myself. You put the Beatles on, I'll put the Undertakers on. It's good for your venue, good for my venue.'

That's what I mean by friendly rivalry. There were two great bands, and the kids themselves could decide whether they would go and see the Beatles one night, the Undertakers the next night.

In Hamburg it was a case of the Beatles competing against themselves, but back in Liverpool they were competing against all the other groups. They all had something about them; you'd respect them for the way they performed, their sound, the material they were playing.

As the Liverpool scene grew and developed, what had been kindling wood suddenly started to kick into flame. Whereas before, you might get an audition band and two bands at a particular venue playing from half past seven to half past ten, suddenly promoters started to come up with other ideas. One example was the Tower Ballroom promotions – the so-called 'Operation Big Beat'. Five or six bands played,

A personal shot of Pete on the Cavern stage in April 1962, taken by a fan. Pete's popularity had grown to the extent where there were requests for him to come to the front and sing. When he did his spot, Paul took over on drums.

Paul and Pete with three of their Liverpool fans.

transport for the kids was arranged, it was like an army manoeuvre. There were 2,000 to 5,000 people you have to control, and it's no longer a case of a couple of bouncers.

The kids flocked in to see the bands. The bands developed as well because instead of one or two bands competing with each other, you had seven or eight bands on stage and when bands play with one another, they're going to perform to the best of their ability.

When we came back from Hamburg, we soon became recognisable in Liverpool because of the sheer impact of our act. We also began to realise that most of the bands that were making the journey to Hamburg were from Liverpool.

So I thought: there must be something special about the Liverpool bands, they're going down so well in Hamburg. Liverpool was a melting pot of talent; I think it was always there, still is, in fact, thirty years on. Liverpool is just a breeding ground for natural talent, musical, literary, whatever.

Before, anything which lived and breathed, as far as the music industry was concerned, didn't happen thirty miles beyond London. Then, when the breakthrough came, record people were suddenly asking, 'Where is this talent coming from? There must be other bands in Liverpool.' All of a sudden the interest of the world was focused on Liverpool.

We were very aware of how big the Liverpool scene was, simply because of the contrast with Hamburg's music scene. When you played in Hamburg, you played in the same club six or seven nights a week. But in Liverpool we didn't have a residency, we were playing five nights a week in five different locations, and we had this younger, teenage audience. There were no drinks, so you had sixteen-year-olds going to the dances.

Another indication of how amazing the Liverpool scene was is that all the different venues were full. If the Beatles were playing at the Casbah, Litherland Town Hall or the Cavern, it didn't mean that the other venues would be empty. They weren't.

I loved the other groups. The fact that we were the Beatles, allegedly the top dogs in Liverpool, didn't mean that the other bands were below us. I had a lot of respect for Ted Taylor. The first time I saw Ted and the Dominoes I was knocked out by the sheer delivery, his voice, the material he was doing.

The Undertakers played a different brand of music, a big sax sound. The Big Three, how could a trio knock that sound out? The drummer singing all the time, the bass player, Johnny Gus, singing, the two of them harmonising together.

They were great bands and I used to enjoy watching them. I would spend a lot of time at the Cavern. It was a meeting place, particularly at lunchtime sessions. But even when we were on the circuit there were certain bands you'd go out and watch because their performance was so great.

The scene in Liverpool was like being part of a growing family. It was expanding all the time and you were always meeting people. You'd play on the same bill as them, you'd bump into them in town or finish after a gig and there'd be a quick pint or off to the bowling alley or Joe's Cafe.

At one point I was placed in front of the others on stage. If memory serves me right, we only tried this once or twice. It was Bob Wooler's idea. He said, 'If you move Pete up to the front instead of him being stuck in the back, the lads would be playing at the side, and everyone's together across the stage.'

We said, 'We'll try it, we'll try anything once, see how it goes.' But when we kicked off, within moments the drum kit was nearly pulled off stage and I wasn't too far behind it! So we had to yank everything back. Bob said, 'Try it one more time and see what happens.' The same thing happened again. Bob said, 'If you keep persevering with it, people will accept it.' I said, 'No, it's too disruptive, I'm just going to go back and play like I normally play.'

The other Beatles were in hysterics at the plight I was in. When things started getting pulled off and I wasn't too far behind, there was raucous laughter from them.

PETE BEST   Photo: Barry Farrell

THE NEARNESS OF YOU

Strange things happen on the Merseyside rock 'n' roll scene, and there are many interesting and unusual stories to be told.

We were recently surprised to hear of the extent to which the magnetic personality of **Pete Best** appeals to girls. Pete, a former member of **The Beatles**, now drummer with **Lee Curtis and the All-Stars** has been responsible for setting many girls' hearts a-flutter in the past.

Recently, several girls have taken to sleeping overnight in his garden—just to be near him! Fantastic!—Yes, but true.

Several eye witness reports tell us that they have seen the girls curled up against a nook in a corner of Pete's garden.

The best of luck to them!

(The above photograph of Pete Best will soon be available in the series of Mersey Beat Photopics. Readers wishing to reserve a copy of the photograph should send a postal order for 1/6d. to the editorial address, and it will be sent to them, post free, on publication).

A story on the fact that fans used to sleep overnight in Pete Best's garden.

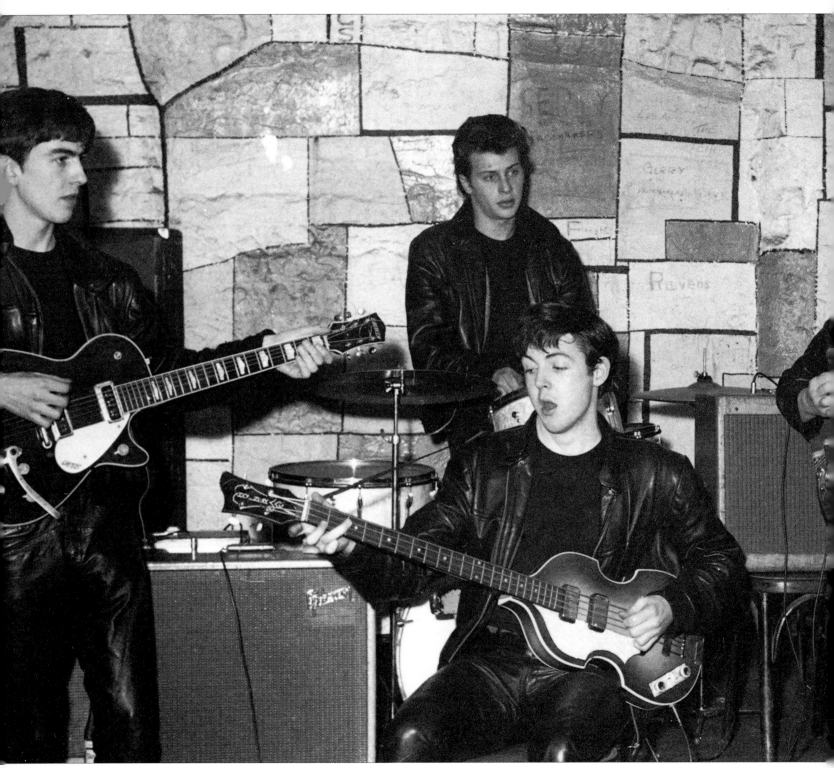

THE BEST YEARS
OF THE BEATLES

14 HAVING FUN

The Beatles were always noted for their high jinks, although they never acted as wildly in Liverpool as they did in Hamburg. After their initial transformation in Hamburg, the competition with other bands in Merseyside had tested their mettle, and they were soon Liverpool's top group. Their sense of humour and Scouse wit was typical of local groups at the time.

At one time John and Paul took pin-up photos of some fans in the back of the van. We always put it down to the fact that after meeting Astrid, they got bitten by the photography bug.

There were some fans in Liverpool who John and Paul had approached and they talked them into posing in the scant – or as close as they could get to it. The fans agreed to it and when it actually happened, it became the high point of conversation that night.

We were playing at the Cavern and in the band room they said, 'Yeah, we just had an afternoon, you know, snapping away: briefs, bras and all the rest of it.' We said, 'How did you manage that?' and 'Lucky buggers. Who was it? Point them out to us'. What we were interested in was having a look at the pictures.

So for the next couple of days they got their ear bent: 'Have you got those photos? Let's have a look at those photos.' And then, when we knew who the girls were, we said to them, 'We know who you are, we know what you did'.

It was a high point in their careers as photographers!

Then there were the Litherland Town Hall gigs, at which Bob Wooler would compère. Bob began to use Rossini's *William Tell Overture* as our introduction; it was the *Lone Ranger* theme tune. He gave us this big intro: 'Dahdahdah da da da da da da – boooooom! The BEATLES!' The minute that this music started, he'd announce, 'Here

Left: The Beatles on stage at the Cavern backing American singer Davy Jones during a lunchtime session on 8 December 1961. They also backed him the same evening at the Tower Ballroom. (Apple Corps)

CASINO
BALLROOM
LEIGH

Announce the Opening of
their New MONDAY NIGHT *Presentations*

IT'S NEMS ENTERPRISES'
Fabulous

"SHOWDANCE"

Featuring
Sensational Opening Attraction . . .

February 25th THE BEATLES

March 4th *Columbia Recording Artistes*
Gerry & The Pacemakers

March 11th Jimmy Crawford & the Ravens
Plus Billy Kramer & the Dakotas

March 18th Brook Bros.

March 25th Karl Denver Trio

Tickets 5/- Available in advance
or on night at Casino Ballroom.
(Except March 25th for which tickets will be 6/-)
JIVING FROM 7-30 p.m. — BE EARLY!

A Bob Wooler Production

Don't Miss This Great Event!
BIG, BIG Monday Re-Opening
at the
PLAZA Ballroom
DUKE STREET, ST. HELENS
MONDAY, 25th JUNE, 1962

Non-Stop JIVE Session — 7-30 to 11-0 p.m.
HARRY BOSTOCK presents his
"BIG BEAT BARGAIN NIGHT"
Starring the North's No. 1 Rock Combo!

THE BEATLES

Just back from their Sensational German Tour
Now Recording Exclusively for Parlophone
They're Terrific — You must see them!
FIRST EVER APPEARANCE IN ST. HELENS
PLUS
The Big Three
Star Group of the JERRY LEE LEWIS "Rockerscope" Show

The Show will
be presented by **BOB WOOLER**
The Well-Known Compere *and* **DEE JAY**
These Fabulous Attractions can only be seen at the Plaza !
TELL YOUR FRIENDS. Come early and see the full Show.

Note the Date
ADMISSION ONLY 2/6 Monday, 25 June
Wilcock-Print.. St. Helens 3868

Two handbills for Beatles gigs at the Casino, Leigh and the Plaza, St Helens. DJ Bob Wooler took a hand in both appearances. He did much to champion the Beatles and he reckons he must have introduced them on stage approximately 400 times. (Sotheby's)

they are: John, George, Paul and Pete!' If there were curtains, they would roll back and the place would just erupt.

They'd be dancing to other bands, but the minute the Beatles were announced, the crowd stopped dancing, the surge came to the front of the stage and very few of them moved while the Beatles were on. By this time they had got to know our names and were shouting and screaming; it was only when we had actually finished that the crowd at the front of the stage would break up and go back to dancing again.

I think the very first gig we did on our return from the Top Ten in Hamburg –

the 'welcome home' gig – was in fact, Mo's. By then we'd increased our price. Mo said, 'Fine, I'll pay it.' I think we made a phenomenal leap from about seven pounds a gig to something like fifteen, which was quite unheard of in those days. We did the 'welcome home' gig at St John's Hall, Snaefell Avenue. St John's Hall was slewin', people battling, and the place went wild.

Bob Wooler had by now become the resident DJ at the Cavern, and we began playing there lunchtime, evening, all-night sessions. Bob was almost always there and he wrote a full-page article in *Mersey Beat* about the revolution which was taking place. He alludes to me in that particular piece as 'mean, moody and magnificent'. The tag 'a teenage Jeff Chandler' emanated from that article. I remember that after the article had appeared I was quite embarrassed about it. When I saw Bob he said, 'It's great, don't worry about it. That's how I see it.'

We were playing the Cavern after that, and someone from the audience who must have read the article in *Mersey Beat* shouted up: 'When's mean, moody and magnificent gonna sing "Matchbox"?' My face went bright red. I remember the rest of them saying, 'It's him, it's him', so I thought to myself, 'OK, it's my turn for the stick now.' But it was a good night, people enjoyed it. Afterwards the tag tended to stick – everywhere you went it was: 'Here's mean, moody and magnificent.' Fans wouldn't allude to me as Pete any more when they went to the Cavern. They'd say, 'It's the three Ms walking round.'

I remember Hambleton Hall because it was an incredible hall. Bob used to DJ us on that one, too.

Hambleton Hall is situated in St David's Road, Huyton, Liverpool 14. The Beatles made their debut there on 25 January 1961 and played a total of sixteen times, making their final appearance on 13 February 1962. The promoter was Vic Anton, who hired Bob Wooler as his resident compère. Affectionately referred to as 'the hive of jive', it was later turned into a probation office.

At Hambleton Hall we did a number called 'Hully Gully' which we had brought back from Germany. We used to do Hambleton Hall regularly on a Sunday night, a fairly rough venue. We'd start 'Hully Gully' and it was the key word that triggered them off – the split second we started playing, all hell broke loose. Everyone started fighting with one another. The first time it happened we thought, 'Ah, maybe it's a one-off.' The next time we were there, everything was quiet. Then: 'Hully Gully', one, two, three, four – boom! The place erupted again. If the Beatles were on, the audience

Paul and Pete with promoter Sam Leach at the Tower Ballroom; the occasion saw Paul introducing Sam as he made his 'singing' debut. The Tower gigs gave the Beatles their biggest local audiences.

This page and opposite: *Mersey Beat* adverts, handbills and a ticket to some of the Tower Ballroom promotions featuring the Beatles. At one time Sam was about to enter a partnership with Brian Epstein to launch shows at the Tower in which the Beatles would support a series of hit recording stars, but Epstein insisted on his brother Clive getting a split. Sam objected, so Epstein took over.

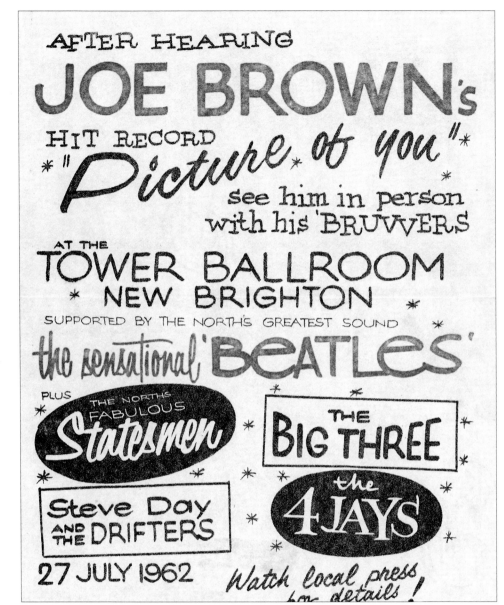

would wait all night for us to play 'Hully Gully', and that was the green light for the barney to start.

Bob began to get a little paranoid about this, because every time we played the number there was a riot in the hall. It wasn't just a couple of people pushing one another, it was the whole works.

So Bob came up to us and said, 'Are you going to play "Hully Gully" tonight?'

THE ROCKING TOWER

BALLROOM, NEW BRIGHTON
LEACH ENTERTAINMENTS
PRESENT

OPERATION BIG BEAT 3

Friday, 29th June, 1962
MERSEYSIDE'S
TOP TEN GROUPS

STARRING PARLOPHONE & E.M.I.
RECORDING ARTISTES

THE BEATLES

SUPPORTED BY
★ The Big 3
★ The 4 Jays
★ Kansas City 5
Kingsize Taylor and
The Dominoes
★ The Undertakers
★ The Searchers
★ Johnny Templars Hi-Cats
★ Lee Curtis & The Detours
ALSO THE SENSATIONAL
LAUNCHING OF A NEW DANCE
CRAZE SWEEPING AMERICA

"THE TRANCE"

LICENSED BARS UNTIL
12-15 a.m.
LATE TRANSPORT
Liverpool and all Wirral areas
Coaches leave St. John's Lane, Lime
Street, 7-30—8-30 p.m.

TICKETS 6/-
Rushworths, Nems, Strothers, Lewis's
and your local record shops.

NOW . . .

SAM LEACH launches the BIGGEST "BEAT" programme ever undertaken

TOWER BALLROOM, NEW BRIGHTON EVERY FRIDAY

FRIDAY, DECEMBER 1st—
THE BEATLES   RORY STORM AND THE HURRICANES
DALE ROBERTS AND THE JAYWALKERS   KINGSIZE
TAYLOR AND THE DOMINOES   DERRY AND THE SENIORS
STEVE DAY AND THE DRIFTERS

FIRST HEAT—"KING TWIST" COMPETITION

7-30 p.m. to 1 a.m.   Licensed Bars (until 11-45 p.m.)

Late Transport (Liverpool and Wirral) - - - Admission 5/-

FRIDAY, DECEMBER 15th—
THE BEATLES   RORY STORM AND THE HURRICANES
DERRY AND THE SENIORS
DALE ROBERTS AND THE JAYWALKERS

QUARTER FINALS—"KING TWIST" COMPETITION

7-30 p.m. to 1 p.m.   Bar   Usual Late Transport

FRIDAY, DECEMBER 8th—
"THE DAVY JONES SHOW"

Starring America's most dynamic "Beat" entertainer
Direct from his "Saturday Spectacular" T.V. show
REPRISE RECORDING ARTISTE

DAVY JONES

with THE BEATLES, RORY STORM AND THE HURRICANES
GERRY AND THE PACEMAKERS, THE REMO FOUR
EARL PRESTON AND THE T.T.s

Britain's leading compere—ALAN ROSS

SECOND HEAT—"KING TWIST" COMPETITION

7-30—2-0 a.m.   Licensed Bars until 12-45 a.m.

Late transport (Liverpool and Wirral)

TICKETS 7/6 (Rushworth's, Lewis's, Strothers, etc.)   At door 8/6

TOWER BALLROOM
NEW BRIGHTON

FRIDAY NEXT
23rd NOVEMBER

12th ANNUAL

ART'S BALL

7-30 p.m.—2-0 a.m.

GRAND FANCY DRESS COMPETITION
Prizes for best original, historical, humorous costumes
★
Licensed bars
★
Transport to all parts of Merseyside
★
TICKETS 7/6
Nurses and H.M. Forces (in uniform) 5/-
Tickets—Usual agencies

3 TOP BANDS

Parlophone Recording Artistes
THE BEATLES

London's Top Jazz Band
THE LLEW HIRD JAZZ BAND

One of Merseyside's Golden Groups
BILLY KRAMER AND THE COASTERS

ALSO FEATURING:—
The Pipes and Drums of 1st. Battalion
Liverpool Scottish Regiment (Queen's
own Cameron Highlanders).

GET YOUR TICKETS NOW ! ! !

BIG BEAT SESSIONS

EVERY FRIDAY at the
TOWER BALLROOM, NEW BRIGHTON
FRIDAY, 1st DECEMBER 1961

Another Great Six Band Line Up -

THE BEATLES - - RORY STORM AND THE HURRICANES
DALE ROBERTS AND THE JAYWALKERS - DERRY AND THE SENIORS
KINGSIZE TAYLOR & THE DOMINOES - STEVE DAY & THE DRIFTERS

First Heat "Mr. Twist" Competition

7-30 p.m. to 1-00 a.m.   Licensed Bars (until 11-30 p.m.)

LATE TRANSPORT (Liverpool, Wirral and Cheshire)
Excursions Leaving St. John's Lane (Lime Street) 7-30 p.m. to 9-00 p.m

TICKETS 4/6

THE TOWER BALLROOM

NUMBER ONE STAR SHOW

starring

★ BRUCE CHANNEL

Hit recorder of "Hey! Baby" and "Number One Man" with Delbert McClinton Harmonica and The Barons

THE NORTH'S No. 1 GROUP

★ The Beatles

of Stage, Radio and Record Fame
making their first Tower Ballroom appearance since their
return from the Star Club, Hamburg

★ HOWIE CASEY

AND THE SENIORS
Fontana Recording Stars

★ THE BIG THREE

★ THE 4 JAYS

★ Compere: BOB WOOLER

Thursday, 21st June, 1962

7-30 p.m. to Midnight
Licensed Bars
Late Transport to all
parts of Merseyside

TICKETS 4/6 now on sale at
Nem's, Rushworth's, Lewis's,
Hessys, Strothers and Tower
Ballroom, etc. (5/6 at door
on night)

A member of the audience takes to the mike while the Beatles are on stage at the Tower.

And we said, 'Yeah.' He said, 'Oh, please leave it out of the repertoire. Don't put it in.' So we said, 'If we don't put it in they're gonna start fighting anyway.' But he said, 'No, try it.' Lo and behold, we did one set without 'Hully Gully' – not a murmur. We put it back in the set and all hell broke loose.

Then there was Knotty Ash Village Hall, which was one of Mo's venues. One night some of the Beatles were on holiday, so I went with Gerry Marsden.

Gerry and I met up for a couple of pints at the Knotty Ash pub. As we were crossing the road, feeling quite merry, all hell broke loose inside the hall. A phenomenal fight started, chairs getting thrown all over the place. Ted Taylor was on stage. In a situation like that, bands usually just keep playing through. But it was a bad fight, a real blood-and-guts one, and I got involved because people were swinging punches at me. As this was going on we looked up at the stage to see if Ted was there, but he'd gone.

Mo was upset because the dance couldn't continue. Everyone had been moved outside the hall, but there was just too much action.

Ted was sitting in the dressing room. Mo said, 'I'll still pay you, Ted. It wasn't your fault. I'm a woman of my word. But I thought you might have stayed out there.' He said, 'Bugger off, Mo. I might be a big feller but I'm not stupid, you know. Let those idiots get on with it, I'll just sit here and wait till it's all over.' And that's what he did.

The first time we did a Cavern all-nighter it was a mixture of jazz and rock bands. We called ourselves rock bands at the time.

When we got there it was just after midnight. We were going on at two or three o'clock in the morning. We were thinking to ourselves, 'There won't be anyone there.' I said to the lads, 'We'll get paid for doing nothing: just turning up and playing numbers.' When we got there the place was knee-deep in bodies. People had come to bed down for the night.

That was the first all-nighter. When we came out of it we thought it was the closest we'd come to the Hamburg experience, where you'd start playing at seven and come home at three o'clock in the morning. I think we finished playing at six o'clock in the morning, when the buses started to run again. We came back out into daylight again, and the birds were twittering away, and we were still bright and breezy and John was saying, 'Where can we go?', 'What's open?' and 'What can we do?'

The all-nighters that followed gradually went over to being all rock, with no jazz. It was like one big party in the band room. People had stacked it up with crates, smuggled in, and were sitting in there drinking.

When the audience came out in the morning it wasn't a case of 'I wanna go to bed.' They were all saying, 'Where can we go?' This mass of people congregating around Mathew Street, all wondering where to go at six o'clock in the morning!

The *MV Royal Iris* was a popular Mersey ferry boat with its own dance floor, which presented regular dances until it was finally taken out of service in the late 1980s.

The 'riverboat shuffle' gigs were first introduced on board by the then Cavern owner Alan Sytner in June 1957. Ray McFall initially introduced the mix of jazz and rock and roll on 25 August 1961, when the bill comprised Acker Bilk's Paramount Jazz Band and the Beatles. Tickets cost 8/6d. The ferry left the landing stage at Liverpool Pier Head at a quarter to eight in the evening, and returned at eleven.

THE CAVERN PRESENTS A RIVERBOAT SHUFFLE

FRIDAY, 25TH AUG. 1961.

ABOARD THE

"M.V. ROYAL IRIS"

WITH

MR. ACKER BILK'S

PARAMOUNT JAZZ BAND

And THE BEATLES

BOAT SAILS AT 7.45 P.M.
FROM LIVERPOOL LANDING STAGE
RETURNING AT 11.0 P.M.

Tickets 8/6

The Beatles were to appear on a total of four shuffles, with Pete appearing on three of them. For their 6 July 1962 gig on the ferry they again appeared with Bilk, who was then in the top ten with 'Stranger on the Shore'. The third shuffle took place on 10 August 1962, when the Beatles appeared with Johnny Kid and the Pirates and the Dakotas.

We went on a riverboat shuffle with Acker Bilk. At this riverboat shuffle, our first, I remember Bilk's drummer saying, 'No need to set two kits up on stage, Pete.' I said, 'Great.' He said you couldn't set two kits up on stage, the crowd was too thick. I didn't realise the drummer was left-handed. I jumped on his kit and said, 'Oh, shit! How do you play a left-handed kit?' But it was a great experience, the first shuffle of its type, and the excitement was there.

Acker Bilk had his hits, so our gig together was the number one band and the number one jazz band playing on the same bill. It was mayhem. The bars were open and the place was packed, with people on the decks because they couldn't get into the middle of it, who were looking through the windows at the bands.

We were in the same changing room as Acker, at the back of the stage. I always remember him saying, 'Come and join us for a drink, come in and we'll both share it.' 'Yeah, OK,' we said, and when we went in there was this mountain of crates right up to the ceiling. He'd stocked himself up. He said, 'Oh, I'm not going to fight for my beer. Dig in.'

I remember there was quite a distinctive swell hitting the *Royal Iris*, so while we were playing we could feel the stage swaying and the people swaying in front of us. The thing was, it wasn't a place you could escape from, you were stuck on board until the ferry docked.

I remember unloading. Neil had the van parked near the Pier Head. He said, 'Oh God, we've got to get off at midnight and carry all our equipment, up or down, depending on what the tide is.' He was talking about the landing stage, which rose or fell with the tide.

It was a fair hike over to where the van was, so we said to Neil, 'See if you can get it a bit closer.' He drove it over the pavements, through the bus sheds and virtually got it on the landing stage, so that we could carry the stuff up and just throw it into the van.

But it was one of those nights when there was no late transport. When we got back up, people who were walking home were asking, 'Can you give us a lift?' So our van, on the way home, was dropping people off like a Number 75 bus. People were hanging out of the windows, the doors were swelling, they were over the top of the kit; you'd open the door and pow! they'd explode out of the van.

On 15 October 1961 a three-hour charity show in aid of the St John Ambulance Brigade took place at the Albany Cinema, Northway, Maghull, Liverpool. It was organised by the late Jim Gretty, then a local theatrical agent, guitarist and salesman at Frank Hessy's, the local music store. There were more than a dozen acts on the bill, mainly local variety performers.

The popular country act Hank Walters and his Dusty Road Ramblers also appeared at the Albany Show. Lennon said to Walters, 'I don't go much on your music, but give us your hat.' Walters told him that the Beatles would never get anywhere playing the type of music they did.

We did a charity matinee show at the Albany, Maghull. Jim Gretty said, 'There's a charity show at the Albany in Maghull – will you do it?' We said, 'Yeah, we'll do it.' He then said, 'Ken Dodd's topping the bill.' 'So what?' we said. We heard afterwards that Ken supposedly didn't want us to appear. So we arrived with our leathers, cowboy boots, just did it as we normally did. There were a variety of acts: people were singing light opera and Jim Gretty was on playing his guitar. Word had got out we were going to appear, and the fans turned up in force.

I suppose you could say it was the first charity show we ever did. We only had ten minutes, so we just did four or five stomping numbers, blasting out, going out in

Pete and Paul pose with singer Emile Ford, hit singer of numbers such as 'Slow Boat to China'. Ford visited the 'Operation Big Beat II' promotion at the Tower and while Davy Jones sang with the Beatles, Ford took to the stage with Rory Storm and the Hurricanes. (Apple Corps)

a blaze. We realised we couldn't do our own fun set and we weren't too concerned where we were on the bill. It was for charity. I think we made a couple of bob for petrol, that's all. We may have been out of place on a bill which had specialist variety acts, but we were well received. I suppose it was our first theatre show in front of a seated audience.

Another fun time was when the Beatmakers appeared at Litherland Town Hall. That was Bob's idea. Gerry and the Pacemakers and the Beatles were both on the same bill.

When we'd played, Bob said what a great idea it'd be to introduce a new band on stage for the first time ever. He put the idea to us and said, 'We'll call it the Beatmakers. I'll introduce it as that.'

Freddie and I played drums, two drums, with Les and the rest of our lads on stage doing 'What'd I Say?'. Since both bands played 'What'd I Say?' it seemed a convenient number to do. Both groups were in the same dressing room and when Bob came and asked if we would mind doing it, we all said, 'No, should be a laugh.'

We were introduced, the curtains opened and there it was, the Pacemakers and the Beatles playing together on stage, the one and only time it ever happened.

The appearance by the Beatmakers took place on 19 October 1961, and the event was duly reported in *Mersey Beat*. Apart from Pete and Freddie Marsden playing drums, Les Maguire played saxophone, Les Chadwick played bass, Paul McCartney played rhythm guitar, John Lennon played piano, and Gerry Marsden and George Harrison were on lead guitar and vocals. Karl Terry and the Cruisers were also on the bill that night and Karl joined the vocalists on stage.

To add to the fun, some of them dressed up. Gerry Marsden wore George Harrison's leather outfit, George wore a hood and Paul McCartney wore a nightie.

They performed three numbers that evening: 'Whole Lotta Shakin'', 'What'd I Say?' and 'Hit the Road, Jack'.

We also backed a couple of hit artists around this time: Davy Jones and Emile Ford. Ford played with the Checkmates at the Tower, but in the afternoon he came to the Cavern.

American singer Davy Jones appeared with the Beatles for the first time at the Tower Ballroom, New Brighton, on 24 November 1961. They also performed with him twice on 8 December 1961, when they backed him during a Cavern lunchtime session and in the evening at the Tower.

We didn't know Davy Jones personally, but were aware of him through 'Amapola', which was his big hit. He was wild, he was incredible. We thought we were wild, but his whole manner – as soon as he walked into a place everyone was vibrating off him.

A cover featuring the Beatles with singer Emile Ford. Incidentally, fellow cover star Billy Kramer used to have weight problems early in his career!

Sam Leach came out with some cracking ideas. He was also involved in the Tower Ballroom. But our first dealings with him were a disaster.

We'd done a couple of gigs for him in and around Liverpool, and he said, 'Pete, you're doing the bookings, aren't you?' I said, 'Yeah, that's me. Tell me what you want, what we can do for you. Sit down at my table, cost you a pint.' This usually used to be done at the Grapes.

So he said, 'Aldershot.' I pointed out it was a long way to travel and he said, 'It's OK, I'll lay on the transport and all the rest of it.' So we said, 'Fine, we'll be getting paid the amount we want, Sam's going to lay the transport on and all we've got to do is go down and play.' So we drove to Aldershot and went to this place. We didn't see any posters up.

'Did you advertise this, Sam?' I asked. 'Yeah, people know about it. It'll be full by tonight,' he said.

We went and had a bite to eat, fish and chips and a couple of pies. The doors opened at half past seven: nothing. When the doors opened, we usually expected the

Backstage at the Tower Ballroom, New Brighton, on 21 June, 1962. Brian Epstein had begun his policy of placing the Beatles second on the bill to hit recording artists to enhance their prestige. This show featured Bruce Channel, of 'Hey, Baby', fame, accompanied by harmonica player Delbert McClinton. Delbert showed John some licks on his harmonica – which may have inspired the haunting harmonica passage on 'Love Me Do'.
(Michael McCartney)

place to be filling up. Eight o'clock: there were only half a dozen people. So we said, 'Shall we go on, Sam? No one's gonna turn up.'

We went on, we did it, but we just totally jested it. I mean, some of us didn't even take our overcoats off. We got off the stage and danced round the floor. The people who were dancing must have wondered what the hell was going on. Here are the Beatles from Liverpool, they're jumping off stage putting their overcoats on and dancing with people. They're not rock and roll – they're doing ballroom dancing. We couldn't have given a toss, and there was no one there to see the antics we were getting up to anyway. We came off, got hold of Sam and said, 'Sam, Sam, what have you done to us?'

'Don't worry, boys, I'll pay you your money.' We said, 'We know you'll pay us the money, there's no problem on that side.' So he said, 'I don't know what went wrong, can't put my finger on it.' But to give him his due, he got a couple of crates of brown ale and said, 'Here you are, if I can say I'm sorry, will this do?' So we said, 'Yeah, fine', and after quaffing the bottles of brown we were ready to get back on the bus and travel all the way back. After that, every time Sam came up to us offering engagements we'd be saying, 'Mmmmm, well, it's Sam.'

The Tower Ballroom gigs, which Sam was involved in, were expansive. You had five or six bands on stage during an 'Operation Big Beat'. I suppose to take it on demanded some bravery, because the Tower's on the other side of the Mersey, in New Brighton, and there's quite a lot of planning to be done with it. A massive ballroom holding 5,000 people.

They'd start at seven o'clock and finish at midnight. So transport had to be laid on. It was quite a manoeuvre to get everyone over there. With something like that, you're either gonna do well out of it, or it's gonna cripple you. It's such a big place.

We'd been to New Brighton as kids, to the fairground. But the Tower itself! When we got inside and saw the size of the stage and the ballroom, which was huge, I said, 'God, what is this?'

Sam Leach was probably the most innovative promoter in Liverpool. It's a pity he didn't have the finance behind him because he would have been able to expand on his ideas. The 'Operation Big Beat' Tower Ballroom promotions he organised took a lot of effort, and virtually set up the infrastructure for late night travel from the venue, which was in a fairly isolated position across the River Mersey from Liverpool. Once he'd established it, Brian Epstein just stepped in and took over.

The Aldershot fiasco took place at the Palais Ballroom on Queens Road, in Aldershot, Hampshire, on 9 December 1961. Once again, the idea behind it was good. Sam believed that Liverpool groups should have exposure in the South, and had intended to get London agents along to see them. But it was rather naive to expect moguls of the calibre of Tito Burns to travel to Aldershot to see unknown bands.

This gig was the first of a series Sam intended to run at the venue, and he'd already booked Rory Storm and the Hurricanes for the following week. The fatal flaw was that the Beatles show was totally unadvertised, and no one in the vicinity knew anything about it. Sam had sent a cheque for 100 pounds to the *Aldershot News* as payment for a large advertisement, but hadn't been aware that they didn't accept cheques from first-time advertisers. They never placed the ad for him.

Sam had by this time already launched his ambitious Tower Ballroom promotions, on 10 November 1961. They were the first of a series featuring a host of Liverpool bands, generally with the Beatles headlining. This was one of the most memorable series of promotions during the *Mersey Beat* years, which have not received the recognition they deserved.

THE BEST YEARS
OF THE BEATLES

15 ▷ EPPY

Group managers on Merseyside were all amateurs before the appearance of Brian Epstein. Simply having a phone or a car provided suitable credentials for someone to take over the management of a group. Management was very much a second job at a time when groups may have had aspirations but the North–South divide was such that few bands from the provinces ever made it – and those that did had to do so by moving to London.

Managers ranged from bouncers to greengrocers. Billy J. Kramer's original manager, Ted Knibbs, was a pensioner. What impressed people about Epstein was the fact that he came from a wealthy family who owned record stores. He was fastidious about punctuality, manners and dress. When he changed the Beatles' image from leather-clad rebels to smart, mohair-suited boys-next-door, he was simply moulding them into the conventional image which suited him.

As I've already noted, the *Mersey Beat* articles on the Beatles first sparked Epstein's interest in the band. He phoned me at *Mersey Beat* and asked me if I could arrange for him to visit the Cavern to see the group. This was set up for lunchtime on 9 November 1961. The group, together with Bob Wooler (Lennon told Epstein he was his father), then met Brian at his Whitechapel office on 3 December. Another meeting followed on 6 December and they all met up at the Casbah on 10 December. The Beatles finally signed a management contract with Epstein on 24 January 1962.

Left: Brian chatting with Billy J. Kramer in the dressing room of the Empire Theatre, Liverpool. Brian initially had a rapport with his artists, but his relationships with Billy, Gerry and Cilla became strained later on. Many fellow managers of the era, such as Colonel Tom Parker, couldn't understand why he didn't devote himself completely to the Beatles, rather than build up a stable of other musicians at a time when he had the hottest property on earth.

When the message got through to us that Brian Epstein actually wanted to see us, we took the time out to go down the road and see who this guy really was.

At that first meeting, Bob Wooler sat in, but very much like a silent partner. Afterwards we decided to take what was said away and mull it over. Which is what we did.

We asked Bob, 'What do you feel about it?' He said, 'What he's laid on the table to you is the fact that he'd like to have a go, he'd like to do something. If it doesn't work, then it's an open-ended agreement. If he can't live up to what he says, or he feels that he can't do it, or you don't like the way he's handling things – finish.' Bob added, 'Just be careful. You're on the verge, there is something happening.'

We went back and talked it over with our parents and explained the position to

A photograph of a young Brian Epstein, given to Bill Harry by Brian's younger brother Clive. Although Brian disappointed his parents in his early years, he eventually vindicated himself by becoming one of the most famous figures of the 1960s.

them, and they all said, 'Fine, if you feel it's the right thing to do, you know we'll support you.'

Mo's advice was very similar to Bob's. She said, 'Fine. There is going to come a time when you need a manager and this man has shown interest.' Whether it was genuine personal interest or it'd been fabricated because of interest from other parties, we didn't know at the time. She also said, 'I can advise, but at the end of the day it's what you feel inside.'

She didn't mean 'you' in the singular, she meant 'you' collectively, as in the band. We decided among ourselves that, yes, we had nothing to lose. When we made the final decision, it wasn't just a case of coming out of the office, going to the pub, having a couple of pints and dashing back to see Brian and saying, 'Yes, you're on.' There was a lot of thought and deliberation behind it.

We knew he was homosexual. People said Brian had been involved in a scandal and he was homosexual and this, that and the other. But at the end of the day we said, 'Well, fine, you know he isn't the first homosexual that we've come across.' We'd come across many in Germany: transvestites, lesbians, homosexuals. Our feeling was that as long as he'd got our interests at heart and he didn't try to get intimate with us, what did we have to worry about?

His circle of friends was his circle of friends, and we said, 'Show business is full of his brand of people; it might even work in our interests.' So we weren't frightened about it.

John was quite laid back about it, actually. At that stage, with typical Liverpool bravado, he said, 'If he lays a finger on me I'll punch his lights out.'

There was one time on the drive to Blackpool when Eppy said to me, 'Would you like to spend the night with me?' and I said, 'No, you've got the wrong guy'. But he didn't persist with it and as far as I was concerned it was done and dusted. He knew where I stood.

John and Cynthia were privy to his offer, simply because they were in the car at the time. There was a little titter from the back seat because I was in the front seat with Brian. So when we stopped off for a drink there was a curious glance across the table, a little smirk on John's face.

In his book *Shout!*, Philip Norman made the allegation that Brian signed us because he fancied John. The suggestion was: 'He'd fallen in love. There he was, mesmerised by these four lads in black leather; they were all good-looking lads.' But it wasn't true.

Brian came down to have a look at us and see what it was all about, who was causing all this furore in Liverpool. Why are these four lads in leather so different from all the other bands?

He'd seen us in Nems, knew that the shop assistants would stop and talk to us. Nems ground to a standstill when we were there. He must have been thinking, 'Does the same thing happen when they're on stage?'

I think Brian was sensible. Rather than just get us to come to the office, or believe the hearsay, he'd gone down to the Cavern, talked to people and seen the reaction. He'd talked to Bob and mulled it over and said, 'I'm prepared to do something with you.'

He wasn't confident, not initially. In fact, he was very nervous while he was explaining what he was trying to do for us. Brian didn't know us, he hadn't talked to us really. He didn't know what the reaction was going to be, whether we were going to be volatile and say, 'Oh, bugger off', or something like that. So I think he was picking his words very carefully as to how he could sell himself to us. He was saying, 'I'd like to give it a go', but I don't think he had any ideas at the time about what route he was going to take.

He told us it would be a two-way thing, that he would take into consideration anything we said. I think that was one of the contributing factors – that he would listen to what we had to say.

Our major consideration at that time was that while we were very big in Liverpool, we wanted to spread out and get a recording contract. We had Polydor, but there were limitations to the Polydor contract. We wanted to record on a major label in our own right and do the things we wanted to do.

This was the first stage, the first thing we had to do. If we got chart success, things will naturally develop from there. And we had a very open discussion with Brian at the time.

We knew it wasn't going to be a case of him taking over and going into overdrive to make us big, because we had the bookings already. We were fully booked up. He hadn't picked a stale band or a group who were only working a couple of nights a week. We were working five, six nights a week, lunchtime sessions, evenings, and starting to move out of town.

Brian began to move us farther afield; soon after we signed with him, he got Mike Smith from Decca to come to Liverpool to see the Beatles – not the Beatles going down to London. He'd convinced this A&R man to come and watch the lads at the Cavern. Things were starting to move fast.

The famous Albert Marrion shot of the Beatles in their black leather. This was part of a studio session taken by Marrion in his Childwall studios – he'd previously been a family photographer for the Epsteins. The shot was used for the front cover of issue No. 13 of *Mersey Beat*. (Albert Marrion)

Mike Smith travelled to Liverpool to watch the Beatles perform on 13 December 1961. He seemed so enthusiastic about their performance that both Brian and the Beatles were convinced they had the recording contract in the bag. An item in the *Liverpool Echo*, written by Tony Barrow, read: 'Decca disc producer Mike Smith tells me that he thinks the Beatles are great. He has a continuous tape of their audition performances which runs for over thirty minutes and he is convinced that his label will be able to put the Beatles to good use. I'll be keeping you posted.'

The fifteen numbers they performed at the session were: 'Like Dreamers Do', 'Money', 'Till There Was You', 'The Sheik of Araby', 'To Know Her Is To Love Her', 'Take Good Care of My Baby', 'Memphis, Tennessee',

'Sure to Fall in Love', 'Hello Little Girl', 'Three Cool Cats', 'Crying, Waiting, Hoping', 'Love of the Loved', 'September in the Rain', 'Besame Mucho' and 'Searchin''.

Incredibly, the Beatles were rejected. And so, perhaps unfairly, Mike Smith's boss Dick Rowe was tagged for the rest of his life as 'the man who turned down the Beatles'.

Smith recorded another band the same day as the Beatles: Brian Poole and the Tremeloes. When Smith approached Rowe for a decision on his two new discoveries, Rowe, perhaps naturally, since Smith had only recently joined the department, said that he could select one of the bands. The Tremeloes were picked — and it does seem likely that it was because they were from nearby Barking rather than the 'far North', as Liverpool was.

Mike watched us at the lunchtime session, and he liked what he saw. We went and had a couple of pints with him at the Grapes. The next thing, we were told, 'An audition's been arranged for you with Decca. Mike will be taking the session and it's on 1 January 1962.' Great!

He also came to the evening session and one of the things he remarked on was the versatility of the music which we played. He also heard us play some original stuff, and intimated to us that when we went down to Decca, we should play the whole spectrum of music and introduce some original numbers. We could harmonise, do out-and-out rockers, sound American, adapt songs and make them fun. After he'd watched us play, Mike had already said, 'I can't see any problems.' He reiterated this after we'd actually put stuff down on vinyl. But it wasn't to be.

It was snowing when we went down to London on New Year's Eve. Neil drove us. Eppy said he'd see us in the studios the following morning.

In those days it was quite a drive down to London. There weren't any motorways. We got there, it was cold and snowing, but we said, 'It's New Year's Eve, we are in London, let's go out and have a few pints and enjoy ourselves.' We got involved in the revelry going on in town, came back, finally got our heads down — and were late getting to the studio the next morning.

By this time Eppy was at the studio waiting for us, and he was frothing at the mouth. I'd never seen him as angry as that. He said, 'What the hell are you doing? This is your big chance, you land up at the studio late, keep people waiting. These are important people.' And John said, 'Ah, bugger off, what's it got to do with you? We're here.' We all agreed with John.

I think it took Brian back a little bit. He was probably thinking, 'They haven't spoken to me like that before.' Our attitude was, 'We're the Beatles. We're late, we accept that. But we're here to do business, and there's no need for you to get on your

One of Epstein's typical sheets of instructions to the Beatles informing them of their local gigs and how they should behave: 'smoking, eating, chewing, and drinking is STRICTLY PROHIBITED.'

```
    9th July  Monday        Plaza Ballroom, St. Helens.
    11th  "   Wednesday     Evening performance at the Cavern
                            Club.
    12th  "   Thursday      Majestic Ballroom, Birkenhead
    13th  "   Friday        Tower Ballroom, New Brighton.


    NOTE!

    26th July Thursday      Cambridge Hall, Southport with
                            Joe Brown.

    27th  "   Friday        TowerBallroom, New Brighton with
                            Joe Brown.

    3rd August Friday       Grafton Rooms, Liverpool
    28th Sept. Friday       Royal Iris River Cruise. (Aut.
                            Telephone Co.)


    NB.

    In the attached copy of 'Mersey Beat' the name 'THE BEATLES'
    on a rough count has been mentioned 15 times.  On the 10
    pages of 'Mersey Beat' 'THE BEATLES' appears on 6 pages.
    There has been a lot pf publicity and there will be more
    and in this connection it will be of vital importance to live
    up to the publicity.  Note that on ALL the above engagements,
    during performances, smoking, eating, chewing, and drinking
    is STRICTLY PROHIBITED, prohibited.
```

high horse and tell us off.' You could tell he was upset, but he masked his feelings once we started playing.

We set up and got ready to go. Once we started playing the music we realised that we only had one or two takes and we had fourteen or fifteen songs to put down. The funny thing is, if you listen closely to the Decca tapes, even though we were blasé about what we were doing, you can still tell that we were trying to hide our nervousness. We knew the occasion was important, but there were mistakes, like people's voices breaking, which wouldn't normally have happened on stage. I know it was an audition and we couldn't go back to put the finishing touches on it, and there was a time constraint — but there is something there and it shows: a little bit of edginess.

We tried a cross-section of our music. That's why, if you listen to it, the recording ranges from Carl Perkins to the Coasters to 'Till There Was You', Peggy Lee type stuff, and original material. From the time we came back from the Top Ten in Hamburg in July 1961, we started to introduce our own material.

Why? Simply because it was great for the egos, great for the public. They were saying, 'What are they playing? It's actually their own songs.' When that was accepted and went down so well, we introduced more original material into the act.

At first I don't think we thought it was stronger. We were interested in introducing it into the act because at that time other people weren't doing original material. I'm not saying there weren't songwriters, but there wasn't a lot of new material getting performed on stage. So it was another feather in our cap to come on stage and say, 'Here is a song which we've written', even though it was mainly stuff which John and Paul had played around with when they were fifteen or sixteen years old.

They'd reached a point where they felt confident and strong enough to start doing it. When it was accepted, people said, 'Hey, they're good songs, we like those', and the requests started to come in for them, to the point where they superseded other material. So when we were going after a record deal, our original material was important. We weren't relying on a studio to say, 'Play this song' or 'Play a cover song.' We had our own stuff.

We also showed our versatility. You had John, who did out-and-out rockers, and then we'd do a slow ballad, such as 'To Know Her Is to Love Her', with the harmony in the background. This was totally different from what John performed on stage – he was the one who was doing 'Twist and Shout' and 'Boys', 'Dance in the Street', 'Rock and Roll Music' and 'Sweet Little Sixteen' with his gravelly pitched voice.

Paul was also showing that he could go from Little Richard style to singing material which was very different, such as 'Till There Was You'. He did it all really well; it was his way of saying, 'I can handle this as well as rock and roll.'

It was a good day, a productive day. The fact that Brian had lost his temper with us was over and done with. Then, when Mike at the end of the session rubbed his hands, thumbs up, and said 'Can't see any problems, you should record. I'll let you know in a couple of weeks', we said, 'We're in!' and 'Let's go and celebrate, do something.' Some of the lads went back with Eppy and I stayed in the van with a couple of the others and came back with Neil. We were all very jubilant, saying, 'Yeah, this is it, we've cracked it.' We were all looking at ourselves and saying, 'What a great way to start 1962, right from day one. Here we go!' Brian kept quiet about the Decca thing but began advertising us as 'Mersey Beat Poll Winners' and 'Polydor Recording Artists'.

I don't really know an awful lot about what happened with the Polydor contract. Brian said he'd had to buy us out of it, get in touch with Kaempfert and say, 'Look, don't hold them to it.'

'My Bonnie' had done well in Germany, but it hadn't set the world alight. But

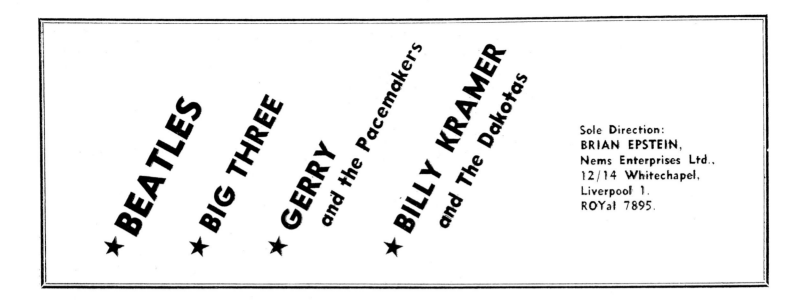

★ BEATLES ★ BIG THREE ★ GERRY and the Pacemakers ★ BILLY KRAMER and The Dakotas

Sole Direction:
BRIAN EPSTEIN,
Nems Enterprises Ltd.,
12/14 Whitechapel,
Liverpool 1.
ROYal 7895.

A *Mersey Beat* advert by Brian Epstein, promoting his stable of acts.

we were billed as the Beat Brothers, so it didn't make any difference – and as it transpires, there were many different line-ups of the Beat Brothers. So what was the problem about getting the Beatles out of the contract?

I had seen Eppy throw a bit of a tantrum if he didn't get his own way. But that didn't wash with us. We'd say, 'Go and sulk, go and throw your tantrum', and I think once he realised it didn't work with us, he stopped doing it.

Our billing as *Mersey Beat* poll winners came about because we'd topped the first *Mersey Beat* poll. Some of us bought lots of copies and filled in several forms; Paul was one of the many who did that. I think every band tried to do it.

Mersey Beat was the music paper everyone was reading, and they were holding a poll to find out from readers who was the number one band. It created a reaction among the readers and among the bands. I remember bands saying, as they were going to gigs, 'I wonder how we're doing in the poll?' and 'When are the results coming out?' It became the main topic of conversation. The poll was just another branch thrown into the fire and it was blazing away.

When *Mersey Beat* held its first poll, it became obvious that various groups were buying copies in bulk to fill in the forms. Together with my girlfriend Virginia, I ran *Mersey Beat*, and when we both counted the entries, the group with the most votes was Rory Storm and the Hurricanes. However, there was a large batch of over forty forms, all filled in green ink in identical handwriting which had all been posted at the same time in the same postal area. We decided to discount these votes. The final order of results was, starting at number one:

MERSEYSIDE'S OWN ENTERTAINMENTS PAPER

MERSEY BEAT

WHY NOT BE A BLOOD DONOR **NOW!**

Please Support
LIVERPOOL ADULT DEAF AND DUMB BENEVOLENT SOCIETY
Parkway, Princes Ave., L'pool 8

VOL 1 NO 4   AUGUST 17 - 31, 1961   Price THREEPENCE

THE BEATLES AGAIN! SEEN HERE DURING THE RECENT ALL-NIGHT SESSION AT THE CAVERN

Photo by Bob Dean

IN THIS ISSUE

FABULOUS PHOTOGRAPHS OF THE BEATLES KENNY BALL GERRY MARSDEN RAY WALKER JOHNNY SANDON RINGO STARR GEORGE HARRISON

1. The Beatles
2. Gerry and the Pacemakers
3. The Remo Four
4. Rory Storm and the Hurricanes
5. Johnny Sandon and the Searchers
6. Kingsize Taylor and the Dominoes
7. The Big Three
8. The Strangers
9. Faron and the Flamingos
10. The Four Jays
11. Ian and the Zodiacs
12. The Undertakers
13. Earl Preston and the TTs
14. Mark Peters and the Cyclones
15. Karl Terry and the Cruisers
16. Derry and the Seniors
17. Steve and the Syndicate
18. Dee Fenton and the Silhouettes
19. Billy Kramer and the Coasters
20. Dale Roberts and the Jaywalkers

From the outset, the Beatles were the most frequent cover stars of *Mersey Beat*.

The second poll appeared in *Mersey Beat* several weeks after Pete had been sacked by the Beatles. He had just joined a fairly new group on the scene, Lee Curtis and The All Stars, who had never featured in the poll before. The evidence of Pete's local popularity was plain when his new band received almost as many votes as the Beatles (who won for the second time), and jumped straight to number two from nowhere.

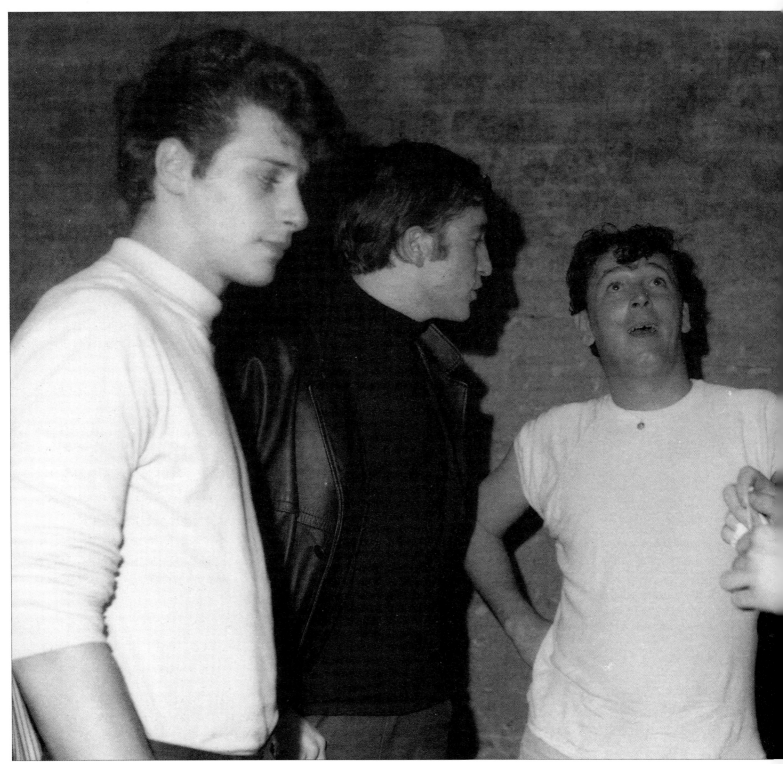

16 ▷ THE STAR CLUB

Manfred Weissleder had vision when he launched the Star Club at 39 Grosse Freiheit – directly opposite the Kaiserkeller, which was by then a strip joint called the Colibri. Not only did he pay top dollar, he also booked the best groups from Britain and America. Naturally, there was a stream of Liverpool groups coming through, from the Beatles to the Searchers, and a host of big American names – Gene Vincent, Little Richard, the Everly Brothers, Bo Diddley, Jerry Lee Lewis.

Manfred hired Adrian Barber, guitarist with the Big Three, to become the club's stage manager, and instructed him to install a sound system which would enable him to record bands live on stage. During tests, Adrian recorded several Liverpool bands, including the Beatles. Manfred recorded groups for his Star Club label, launched a magazine – the *Star Club News* – and began to open Star Clubs in different German cities.

Horst Fascher was sent to Liverpool in January 1962 to book the Beatles for the club's opening season from 13 April to 31 May. The opening bill was the Beatles, Tex Roberg, Roy Young, the Graduates, the Bachelors, the Tony Sheridan Quartet and Gerry and the Pacemakers.

There were all sorts of incidents we got involved with when we went back to Hamburg the third time, to appear at the new Star Club. We'd get drunk and get up to no good, and we wouldn't think anything at all about it. It just happened.

The waiters were the ones who would recall all the antics you had got up to if you couldn't remember them. One of us would stagger into the Star Club and a waiter would say, 'This is what you got up to last night.' In my case, 'So what?' was the answer.

There were so many bands going to Hamburg by this time that it was like a herd. We'd normally stick together. There'd be times when I'd disappear for sticks or skins or to buy another cymbal, but everyone knew that during the day we frequented the

Left: Pete, John, Gene Vincent and Paul. The Beatles were delighted to be appearing with their idol at the Star Club. Apprehensive at first about Vincent's reaction to their leather outfits, they all soon became good friends. (Michael McCartney)

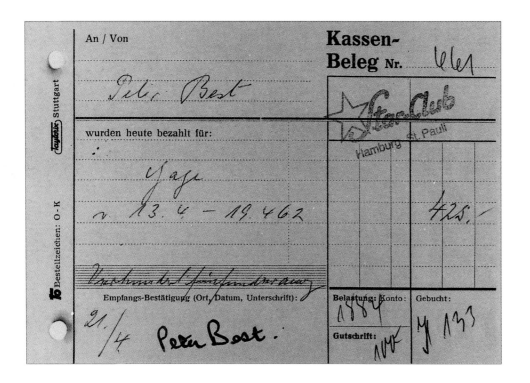

One of Pete's Star Club bills.

same haunts and even if we temporarily disappeared, if you went back to Harold's or the Seamen's Mission, you'd bump into the lads.

I was there when John peed over the nuns. This time we were living in an apartment. Manfred and Horst had put us in the apartment over the road from the Star Club. It had a balcony and we were often out there swilling beer. There was a church opposite, and the nuns would walk up and down a couple of times on this particular side of the street. We bet John, saying, 'You wouldn't piss over them.'

John was that type you shouldn't bet to do anything. The nuns were walking past – and John peed on them over the top of the balcony, just like 'raindrops keep falling on your head'. If it was anyone else they would have run up the stairs and thrown John off the balcony.

We fell about laughing over it, but were told afterwards by Manfred, 'If it happens again, regardless of who you might be, how big you think you are in Germany, you'll be on the next plane back home.'

When the Star Club opened, the *bierfrau*, Bettina, took an enormous liking to John. She was friends with everyone, a big bubbly type of person who would talk to us, laugh and joke. But she'd tell us, 'John is for me. John is my man', and we used to wind John up about it.

We'd say, 'Bettina's waiting for you', and he'd say, 'How can I get out?' Bettina's bar position was at the back door against the back wall, and there were only two ways to get out: the aisles up the side of the staircase which led to the balcony and the back door below the recess. So Bettina had a panoramic view of everyone coming and going.

There'd be times when he'd escape, and times when he'd stay behind. He'd say, 'No, you go and tell her that I've gone missing.' It was just that she loved him so much, she just wanted to be all over him. She wanted him to sit there and drink beer so she could just look at him.

I didn't take prellies like the others. I fired on booze and schnapps, that kept me pumping along. I was used to slugging the drums away, just keep rolling and rolling on; that was my metabolism. I didn't need them. If any of the lads needed them, rather than go out they'd see Mutti. They'd come back ready to play all night . . . and the next day . . . and the day after that.

'Prellies' referred to Preludin, a type of amphetamine that was freely available in Hamburg at the time. Rosa, or 'Mutti', the *toiletten-frau* at the Star Club who'd virtually followed the Beatles from venue to venue in Hamburg, used to have a large jar of prellies which John would dip into. Bettina, at her position in the bar, had a large photograph of John on her wall, captioned 'prelly king'.

Horst Fascher was also at the Star Club. The first time I met Horst was on our first trip out to Germany and he was a waiter. He loved us, got to know us. Then we found out from people that he'd supposedly served a prison sentence for manslaughter. But our first impression of him was that he just liked everything about us and took great pleasure in introducing us to his brothers.

He moved from the Kaiserkeller to the Top Ten, where he was working for Peter Eckhorn. We saw him there and he had the reputation of being a hard guy. We saw him prove this on certain occasions and he was always looking after us.

The Star Club was owned by Manfred Weissleder, but Horst took over the managership of the club. He came over and talked to Brian and booked us to open the Star Club.

When we had to leave Hamburg that first time, Horst was very upset. Then, on our second visit, when we did the three months at the Top Ten, he was there. He saw us every night, used to eat with us, drink with us, laugh and joke with us, and when we were leaving to go back to Liverpool, the first time that we were all leaving together, he was in tears. Here was this outgoing man who had the reputation for being hard and could handle himself, openly shedding tears over the fact that his boys were leaving Hamburg and he didn't know when he'd be seeing them again.

Then there was the delight on his face when he was in a position to come to Liverpool and negotiate with Epstein to open the Star Club. And while he was here for a short spell we got drunk together and he said, 'I can't wait to see you in Hamburg.'

When we got there he was managing the club and had a lot of responsibility. He was very proud of it, but he hadn't really changed. His new position meant he'd gone up in the world, and the Star Club was the biggest thing happening in Hamburg at the

THE BEST YEARS
OF THE BEATLES

time – and he'd been instrumental in it. Yet he still wanted to be one of the boys, when time would allow.

He had this big American Cadillac with enormous wings on it. When we first saw it, we said, 'Good God, look at the size of this, give us a go in your car, Horst!' He thought the world of us and would do whatever he could to make sure we were all right. If there were any problems, whether it was fights or anything like that, he'd say, 'You don't sort it out. I'll sort it out.'

When we went to the Star Club it was the first time we'd flown out to Hamburg, and we were quite elevated by that. Also, this time Stuart and Astrid were actually going to be at the airport to meet us.

We played the Casbah the night before we flew out, in a farewell performance. It was an impromptu performance on a Sunday night.

Sunday was a good day for me and the family to run out to Southport, get some fresh air, walk round the beach. Then we said, 'We've got to get back home, get the club ready.' We were expecting a pretty good crowd. By five o'clock, there was a queue of people outside the gate. Some shouted, 'Hi Mo, going to be a good night', while we made them move over so we could put the van in the back.

I remember Mo sticking her head

Opposite: When the Star Club opened in 1962, it drew lots of young people into the St Pauli red light district. Youngsters up to the age of eighteen were allowed out until a ten o'clock curfew came into force. Night-time audiences comprised a varied crowd of sailors, strippers, rockers and members of the general public out for a good time.
(Pan-Foto/Günter Zint)

out of the kitchen door and shouting, 'We can't let you in until seven o'clock, you know. It's a bit early for you, but amuse yourselves, we'll be with you. We know you're there.' Even so, Mo opened half an hour early; she said, 'Can't keep them waiting outside.' There was pandemonium; by half past seven it felt as if the walls were expanding.

George said, 'I'm not feeling too good', so he didn't fly out to Hamburg with us – he came down with German measles! So it was two or three days before he could fly out to meet us, a couple of days after the Star Club opened.

When we got to the airport, we were very much surprised to find that Stu wasn't there. We asked what had happened and Astrid said Stu had died. She said that he'd had a brain haemorrhage. It left us totally shocked. It was the first time I'd actually seen John physically break down. Because he was such a strong person, he usually kept his feelings and emotions to himself.

We were very sorry, but we knew we had a job to do as well. We were very sympathetic towards Astrid and I think she appreciated that. She said, 'Yes, I know it's bad news but do what you have to do.'

Because there was this wailing harmonica put into 'Love Me Do', people attribute it to the fact that John was lamenting Stu's death. I don't think it was that. It was a new sound, a new experiment, that was it.

There was a change in Astrid. There is bound to be when somebody you love dearly dies. It affects people in different ways, but you could see she was trying to put on a brave face. Even though Stuart had died she came and watched the band. She said, 'I still enjoy the music, you're still my favourites.'

When we arrived at the Star Club, Horst had said that Gene Vincent was coming to the club and we said, 'God . . . Vincent! One of our heroes – and here we are in our leathers. What's he gonna think of us wearing leathers?'

Vincent came along and the first time we saw him, he was just a normal guy, wearing a jacket and tie. Ugh! We thought he was going to eat, sleep, drink in *his* leathers.

When we'd done our bit, Vincent came on wearing his leathers. The way he looked at it, it was just a funny coincidence – 'Does everyone wear leathers in this business?' We said, 'Yeah, but our leathers are better than yours!' We became good friends. We realised that the barriers had broken down, that you could go up and talk to this guy and he'd say, 'I'm going for a beer, are you coming?'

It was quite an experience. We'd played with an American star before – Davy

Jones – but that was a one-off. Here, we were playing at the same club, on the same bill, doing the same things. In a letter home I wrote: 'Gene Vincent's playing at the Star Club, and we're playing on the same bill as him. He's playing our requests. Anything we want, he sings. And he likes us, he likes the music we play and we sing some of his numbers.' The fact that we sang some of his songs didn't worry him. He was interested in the way that we played them. He was sitting in the audience, which he did a lot, rather than hanging around backstage, and he'd sit there and watch our show. We'd say, 'Here's a Gene Vincent number' and he'd wave his fingers in the air.

I think Vincent was more excited about being in Hamburg than we were. Not so much about the fact that we were the Beatles; he'd heard about us because Horst had told him that we were a good band from Liverpool, a great bunch of lads. But I think it was because it was Vincent's first time in Hamburg, and he was as excited about what was going on around him as we'd been on our first trip.

Gene Vincent was a genuine hero of the Beatles. John Lennon and Stuart Sutcliffe together attended the Liverpool Stadium concert on Tuesday, 3 May 1960 which Vincent headlined. Pete Best was also in the audience. At that time the group included 'Be-Bop-A-Lula' in their repertoire. From 1961 they also began to perform 'Dance in the Street' and 'Over the Rainbow'.

The Beatles met and appeared on the bill with Vincent during their seven-week Star Club season. During this time Little Richard, another of their seminal influences, also appeared at the club.

Several weeks after their return to Liverpool, the Beatles appeared with Vincent once again, this time on their home turf when both acts appeared at an evening session at the Cavern Club on 1 July 1962.

17 ▷ NEW IMAGE

Brian Epstein's urge to remake the Beatles in a new image tended towards the conventional. The shiny mohair suits were an attempt to make the group acceptable to the general public, as were the admonitions – sent via typed memos – reminding the band members not to smoke or swear on stage. Brian even tried to cut down on the intimacy the Beatles had with their fans, particularly those who requested songs. John Lennon was always swift to put Brian down if he felt he'd gone too far.

Harry Watmough, a *Mersey Beat* photographer, captured the homogenised, besuited Beatles in a series of photographs. Brian's attempts to ensure that nothing would mar the new image of his dapper young men extended to sending John Lennon to the *Mersey Beat* office on a secret mission. The object was to recover copies of photos from Hamburg, given by John to me, which included pics of John in his underpants in the Reeperbahn, and on stage with a toilet seat around his neck.

Perhaps Brian was genuinely unaware that a revolution was going on, with youngsters choosing their own heroes and fashions. The Beatles' fans had already voted for the leather-clad image with their feet – by packing out every venue the group appeared in.

Fortunately, the talent and uniqueness of the Beatles transcended the change. Brian's ironing out of their rough edges may even have contributed to their success; it is difficult to say. If we were to imagine a situation in which the group stayed in black leather, would this have excited youngsters internationally even more? We'll never know – but it would have nipped the Rolling Stones in the bud!

I felt that in some ways, Brian was gradually changing the group from John's group into Paul's group. John was the aggressive rocker, Paul loved the show business aspect. The changes Epstein made irritated John and delighted Paul.

Our following grew. The German one was different from the Liverpool version. Living in the St Pauli area, you mixed and rubbed shoulders with the German audiences on a more regular basis. You were there six or seven hours a night, and they may have been watching us for four or five hours. We'd talk to them, we'd see them in the street.

Once the impact hit Liverpool, after the Litherland appearance, a phenomenal reaction began. But it wasn't like in Germany; in Liverpool it was more adulation.

Above, opposite and overleaf: Harry Watmough's photos of the smart new Beatles in their mohair. Pete and John hated the new look and pined for their leathers. John, George and Paul have their hair brushed down; no one ever asked Pete to adopt the moptop style.
(Artrock)

German fans would say, 'Hello, you coming for a beer?' In Liverpool it was, 'Can we touch you?' 'Can we talk to you?' or 'Can we come into the band room?' We usually said, 'Fine, we'll talk to you outside.' I think we had a rapport with them, we were approachable, we went and sat and watched other bands.

We had a flexible set because we took in a lot of requests from fans. But Epstein wanted to change all that. He would say, 'You must play this set.' We'd tell him, 'You're not taking into consideration that there are going to be people in the audience who want to hear that number.'

When we went on we didn't know what we were going to do. It all fell into place on stage. John would say, '"Sweet Little Sixteen".' Paul would say, 'I'll do "Kansas City".' George would say, '"Glad All Over"', or 'And now an Everly Brothers one', or '"Feet's Too Big"', or something like that.

It was a random selection, and if someone shouted up from the audience for 'Over the Rainbow' we'd do it. And if somebody else shouted, 'Do "Honey Don't"', we did it because to our way of thinking we were giving the people who came to see us what they wanted to hear.

When Brian tried to make us more clean-cut, or I suppose make us a little more professional, he didn't see it our way. Yet he had to listen to us when we said, 'No, there are certain numbers which we've got to incorporate into our show because fans expect it.'

It was then that he became a bit more liberal in his choice of music. He was still saying, 'You mustn't smoke, you mustn't drink on stage', but he didn't insist on making us play a certain set list when we felt it wasn't going to work.

Brian made us wear suits from Beno Dorn, a tailor. In fact, it was my only suit: a silk mohair dark blue suit with a little weave in it. We went over the Mersey to this tailor after much persuasion, and got measured up. We paid fifteen pounds each for them, which was quite a lot of money in those days. And then we asked, 'What do you wear with it?' That was, of course, a white shirt and black tie. The style made us look commonplace.

John and I hated going into suits. It was, I suppose, because we loved our leathers. We ate, slept, drank in them; that's what they were there for. We loved the image we had, the pseudo-macho thing. We didn't go round proclaiming, 'This is the

Beatles, this is the way we dress, these are the leather jackets, these are our Cuban-heeled boots.' But the outfits were readily identifiable. And we felt that the image was working; no one had said, 'My God, these guys would look far better in suits.'

Some time after Epstein told us his reason for the change, the argument in favour of suits. He said that at that time most bands in Liverpool had adopted a more casual image on stage. So our wearing suits would make us stand out.

When Epstein suggested that we go into suits, John and I were the last to come to terms with it. Our feeling was, 'We can put up with what you're doing: cleaning us up, making us more professional in our outlook, grooming us if you like, but we still don't like the idea of the suit image. We will do it, but we're not happy with it.' Everyone came to terms with it eventually, but there was this awkward changeover period.

What sticks in my mind is that Eppy always wanted to be accepted as one of the boys, as part of the team. As fast as he changed us into suits – which was not our image off stage – he began changing himself. Off stage we were still the same, but whereas before he'd be in a suit and tie, he'd then be the one to roll up in leathers and a polo-neck

sweater or a pair of jeans or slacks. I'm not saying everyone wasn't happy – Paul was happy going into suits and all the rest of it.

But I thought, 'We're still going to generate the same excitement, the same atmosphere whether we're in leathers or suits, so why have we got to go into suits?'

Epstein booked us for a big bash in Port Sunlight and insisted it was a 'wear your suits again' event. He said we couldn't wear leathers, that it was a dinner, a black-tie job. He said, 'You're not going to get the same people who normally follow you around.' It was to be a swish do in the village itself. We were working on the set that we were going to do and Brian would come up with some suggestions. We told him, 'No, no, we're going to do this, we're going to play what *we* want this time.'

Having been assured by Brian that there wouldn't be any of our normal following, we got out into the reception area where the dinner was taking place and – how they got tickets to it, I don't know – but the fans were there! If they wanted to get to a place, they got to it. There were tables with our fans sitting there, still in their duffle jackets and polo-neck sweaters, and further down the hall are all these people in penguin suits and evening dresses.

We tried to keep Brian backstage so he wouldn't see it. I said, 'Think there'll be a bit of a surprise for you tonight, Brian.' He said, 'No, no, no. Everything's in order.'

So we went on in suits, knowing that there were quite a lot of fans out there. The curtains went back, and this scream went up from our fans. Brian was saying, 'What is this?' But the funny thing is, and this took us by surprise, that the people in the penguin suits and lounge suits and evening dresses were rowdier than our fans were. They were the first to get on the floor, the first to run down to the stage. It was probably one of the few occasions we played where our hardcore of fans got pushed to the back.

We came off and told Brian, 'You and your penguin suits and your lounge suits. We won't get the same reaction? Look at that! Even our fans got pushed into a corner.'

He said, 'OK, I put my hand up, you're right.'

Port Sunlight, 'over the water' from Liverpool, was a village created a century ago by Lord Leverhulme, the soap baron. The venue the Beatles appeared at was Hulme Hall in Bolton Road, a Tudor-style building which held rock and roll dances on Friday evenings. The group appeared at the Golf Club Dance on 7 July 1962. At that time Brian was trying to go upmarket, and book them into places he considered more sophisticated than their usual haunts.

18 ▶ MORNING WITH EPSTEIN

When Pete was asked to meet Brian Epstein at his office at Nems in Whitechapel on the morning of 14 August 1962, he had no idea of what it was about, and certainly no inkling of the coming trauma. He was the member of the Beatles who most often met Epstein at his office to discuss arrangements for bookings, as Neil Aspinall, their driver and road manager, also lived with the Bests. Epstein confessed that he had had a sleepless night. No other member of the band elected to be present at the meeting. It was a *fait accompli*, as Ringo Starr had already been engaged to take over the drumseat of the group at the Horticultural Society Dance at Hulme Hall, Port Sunlight on 18 August.

We were at the Cavern when Epstein came up and said, 'I'd like to see you in the office, Pete, around about half past ten.'

On the way home Neil said, 'What're you doing tomorrow?' 'Oh, I've got to see Eppy in the morning,' I said, so Neil said, 'I'll run you there, no problem.'

When we got to the shop next morning Neil said, 'You go upstairs, I'll hang around downstairs.'

I went up to the office. Eppy said, 'Pete, I have some bad news for you. The boys want you out and it's already been arranged that Ringo will join the band on Saturday.'

There wasn't any explanation given. It was left to me to ask, 'Why? What have I done wrong?' There was no forewarning. My brain just went into reverse, was still trying to come to terms with it.

The reason he gave was that 'George Martin felt you weren't a good enough drummer', and that was it. I said, 'That doesn't really make sense, but there's nothing I can do about it because it's already been organised. I mean, Ringo's joining the band.'

Then I asked, 'Where are the others? Why aren't they here so I can ask them?' And that's when he said, 'They've left it to me as the manager of the group to do the dirty business.'

I was under contract, but the contract that was signed at Hayman's Green was the one that Brian had refrained from signing. When it was queried, he said he hadn't

The famous *Mersey Beat* cover proclaiming the Beatles as number one group in the north-west of England. Epstein was able to use the poll results in his promotions.

signed because it still gave us an opportunity to drop out if he hadn't succeeded with the Beatles.

There was a phone call while I was there and when he answered it, Eppy said, 'I'm still with him at the present moment.' I don't know who phoned, it could have been anyone. I wasn't paying too much attention to who was phoning, as I was still trying to fathom the situation.

Neil was the first to see me when I came down and he took one look and said, 'What's happened? You're not the same guy that went up. You bounced up there and now you're dragging yourself out.'

I told him and Neil said, 'What do you want to do?' He meant, 'Do you want to go home or do you want to go for a pint or something and chat about it?'

The other person we ran into that morning was Wally from the Hurricanes, who we bumped into outside Nems. He said that I looked depressed and asked, 'What's happened?' Neil and I, together, said I'd been kicked out of the Beatles and he said, 'I don't believe it.'

We then decided to go to the Grapes, just to sit there and have a pint. Wally said he'd come with us. I wasn't inclined to discuss what happened fully in front of Wally, though. He was a good friend and all the rest of it, but I just said, 'I'm still trying to get it straight in my own head.'

We had some drinks and Wally said, 'I still can't believe it's happened, but wait and see', and then left. But I couldn't help feeling that he'd known about it because Ringo was joining on Saturday and Wally must have heard.

When I got home Neil said to Mo, 'Do you know what's happened?' She said, 'What's the problem?' That's when I sat down and told her.

It had been agreed with Epstein that there were three gigs on two dates to play, the Thursday and Friday before Ringo joined the band, and Eppy had said, 'Would you play them?' In the office, in a state of shock, I said, 'Yeah, I will', but by the time I got home when things had started to sink in, I said, 'I'm not going to the gig. I couldn't play with them knowing this has happened and I'm out.'

So Neil said, 'Can't blame you.' Then he said, 'If that's the way they want to be about it, I'm finishing. I don't want to be part of it.' But I said, 'No. It's happened to me, but they're going places, you can't just jack it in.'

Epstein had the Big Three on the same bill on those two occasions so when I never turned up, Johnny Hutchinson played those couple of gigs. It may have been the case that Eppy had booked the Big Three because he'd expected it and was covering himself.

When Mo heard that it was George Martin's name which had been mentioned, she said, 'Let's go to the horse's mouth.' She got in touch with George Martin and he said, 'Mrs Best, I never said that. I wasn't instrumental in getting rid of Pete. What I said was: "What I hear isn't what I hear on the record in this present moment of time."' He mentioned the fact to Brian, but said, 'Don't break up the physical content of the band, because Pete is such an integral part of that.' He was 'of course surprised' when he was told that I had left the band and said it was as much of a shock to him as to everyone else. People say I wasn't even told the results of the Decca audition. For some reason Eppy didn't tell me, I found out by accident.

Mike Smith had told us we should hear the results of the Decca audition fairly quickly. At the time it seemed to be in the bag. As time elapsed – a couple of weeks went by – I thought, 'Hang on a minute, we haven't heard anything from Mike. Eppy

When Epstein informed Pete that he'd been sacked, the band still had three gigs to play before Ringo joined them – at the Riverpark Ballroom on 16 August 1962 and the Majestic Birkenhead and Tower Ballroom the following night. Naturally, Pete didn't want to do them. Epstein hired Johnny Hutchinson of the Big Three to sit in with the Beatles at the gigs. Epstein had offered Hutchinson the job permanently, but he'd turned it down. Hutch was to say, 'Brian asked me to join the Beatles and I said, "I wouldn't join the Beatles for a gold clock. There's only one group as far as I'm concerned and that's the Big Three. The Beatles can't make a better sound than that, and Pete Best is a very good friend of mine. I wouldn't do the dirty on him."'

Once the news of Pete's sacking was announced, pandemonium broke out on Merseyside and letters poured into the offices of *Mersey Beat*. Pete himself received shoals of fan mail, typified by this letter from May and Christine.

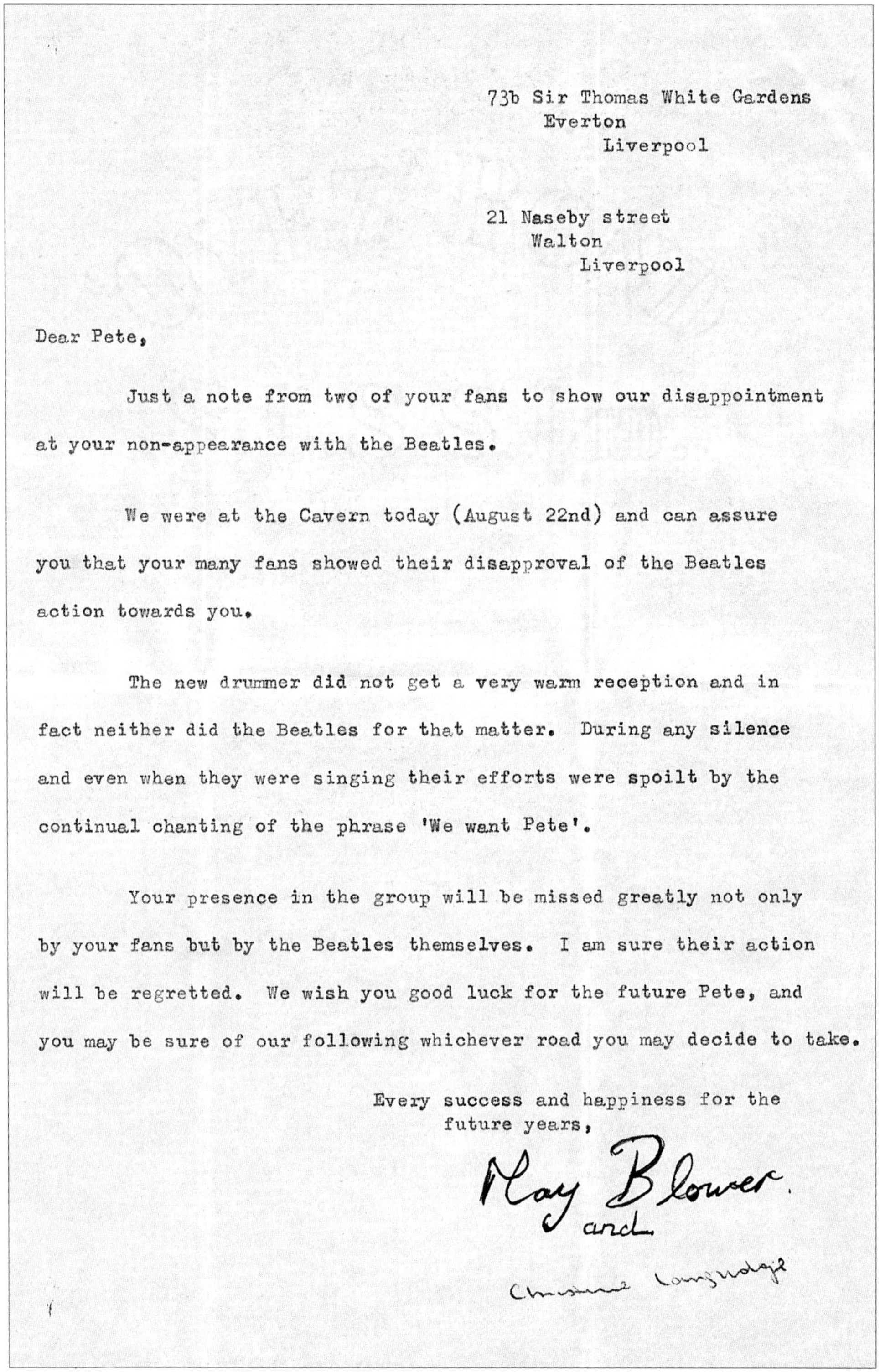

73b Sir Thomas White Gardens
Everton
Liverpool

21 Naseby street
Walton
Liverpool

Dear Pete,

Just a note from two of your fans to show our disappointment at your non-appearance with the Beatles.

We were at the Cavern today (August 22nd) and can assure you that your many fans showed their disapproval of the Beatles action towards you.

The new drummer did not get a very warm reception and in fact neither did the Beatles for that matter. During any silence and even when they were singing their efforts were spoilt by the continual chanting of the phrase 'We want Pete'.

Your presence in the group will be missed greatly not only by your fans but by the Beatles themselves. I am sure their action will be regretted. We wish you good luck for the future Pete, and you may be sure of our following whichever road you may decide to take.

Every success and happiness for the
future years,

May Blower.
and
Christine Langridge

THE NORTH'S OWN ENTERTAINMENTS PAPER

MERSEY BEAT

FRANK HESSY
Limited
62 STANLEY STREET
(Corner of Whitechapel)
LIVERPOOL, 1
FOR ALL MUSICAL INSTRUMENTS
OUR EASY TERMS ARE "EASIER"

Vol. 2 No. 34   NOVEMBER 1—15, 1962   Price THREEPENCE

LEE CURTIS AND THE ALL-STARS
Photograph by Peter Kaye

STOP PRESS

Pete Best with All-Stars

Pete Best, former drummer with The Beatles, is now a member of Lee Curtis and the All Stars. His first appearance as a member of the group will take place on Monday, September 10th at the Majestic Ballroom, Birkenhead. Full story next issue.

MAJESTIC BALLROOM
CONWAY STREET, BIRKENHEAD
FIRST APPEARANCE OF
PETE BEST with
LEE CURTIS & ALL STARS
MONDAY, SEPTEMBER 10th

Above and left: A *Mersey Beat* story announcing Pete's new band. When Epstein had sacked Pete he then suggested that he could sign up the Mersey Beats and make Pete their drummer, but Pete turned him down. There were numerous offers from other bands – it was even suggested that Pete replace Ringo Starr in Rory Storm and the Hurricanes – but Pete eventually joined a relatively new band, Lee Curtis and the All Stars.

hasn't told me or the band about it.' So I asked him, 'Have we heard from Decca?' and he said, 'Yeah, but we didn't get the job. But I'm still persevering and contacting other people.'

Legend has it that I wasn't told – and that I wasn't told about Parlophone, either. People assume from that that things were going on behind my back.

In their efforts to find reasons why I was sacked, some people also point to the hairstyle. They say, 'The other three had what later became the Beatle moptop, but Pete hasn't, so he wasn't going to change his hairstyle.' As I've said, the truth was that no one asked me to change it. It's a fact that when Ringo joined the band, he did have that hairstyle, but someone must have said, 'Do it.'

At that time, the difference in our hairstyles wasn't really noticed. From what I remember, there was a mixture of styles among young people. You have only to look at the photographs of the kids who were queuing up outside the Cavern. I'd gone into suits, gone into leathers, cowboy boots and this, that and the other, done everything to conform to the group's overall needs and requirements. So I would have adopted the hairstyle, too.

People also allege that I didn't mix with the others, while Ringo did. This is also untrue. The affinity which grew in Hamburg carried back to Liverpool. We would still all meet up, we'd still all be at the Cavern lunchtime sessions, we would still all go to the Grapes for a pint.

There were times when, because the van was going back to Hayman's Green, I'd jump into it and say, 'I'm off' because I knew I'd have a lift back home. Sometimes they'd be in the van and they'd come back to Hayman's Green, too.

I don't know where the idea came from that I was a loner and didn't mix. It wasn't a case of detaching myself. We were a unit and that's what people saw all the time. When we were off stage, when we were eating, drinking, laughing and joking, when we were causing bloody riots even on stage, when we were going with women – the group was all there, there was an affinity.

Then something which I'd never heard before cropped up on the *Anthology* TV series about the Beatles. It was unreliability. All of a sudden it's, 'Pete never turned up for gigs.' Now what had I done to deserve this one? Apart from the two occasions when I didn't turn up after I was dismissed, there were only a couple of occasions in the two years when I couldn't make a gig. Once I had to go to court and I told the others in advance; and the other time was when I had 'flu and they were doing a double show at the Cavern. I missed the afternoon session and hauled myself out of my sick bed to do the evening one.

They were the only times.

The year in which Brian Epstein and I had the closest association was 1961. I was the first person from the Mersey scene to contact him directly when I asked him to stock copies of *Mersey Beat* at Nems in July 1961.

Brian was intrigued by the content of the paper and amazed that such activity was taking place on his doorstep. He would visit the *Mersey Beat* office to deliver ads personally and loved to discuss activities in the local music scene.

He was considerate and charming. When he went abroad for a weekend he dropped into the office with a box of chocolate liqueurs for my girlfriend Virginia. On his birthday he invited Virginia and me, together with Bob Wooler, to join him for dinner at the Royal Restaurant. He used to invite me to his office for a sherry to discuss the group scene and it was no surprise when he asked me if I could arrange for him to visit the Cavern to see the Beatles.

When he handed me a typed statement that Pete was leaving the group, I was shocked, but accepted the story Brian gave. He wrote: 'The Beatles comment "Pete left the group by mutual agreement. There were no arguments or difficulties, and this has been an entirely amicable decision."' I had been used to dealing with the truth when reporting about groups, and a great deal of trust was involved. At the time I had no reason to doubt his veracity.

Brian was clever and sophisticated, and found it fairly easy to impress the young people involved in the Mersey scene. Yet, although he ran a music store, his tastes didn't venture into rock and roll and he couldn't tell a good group from a bad one. The publicity in *Mersey Beat* overwhelmingly centred on the Beatles – so when he decided on management, they were the group he set his sights on. He was also to sign up Gerry and the Pacemakers when they were number two in the poll, and Billy J. Kramer when he was voted number three in our second poll.

The sacking of Pete had its repercussions. The fact that he was the most popular member of the Beatles with the Liverpool fans can't be disputed – the copies of *Mersey Beat* from those times prove it. When it was announced that the group had signed with Parlophone, a photograph of Pete Best alone graced the cover. A cover caption read: 'Congratulations to Pete, Paul, John and George and the boys on their successful engagements in Germany.'

As we've seen, in Bob Wooler's prophetic article on the group, the only member mentioned by name was Pete Best. And when the group made their radio debut in Manchester, it was Pete who was mobbed by the fans there.

There was also great appreciation locally for his drumming ability. He put the beat in the Beatles, and some people were even referring to the group as Pete Best and the Beatles.

When I interviewed Pete at the time of his sacking, he was thoroughly confused by it all. No member of the group had ever contacted him to explain why he'd been sacked. The message from George Martin denied that he'd suggested Pete should be sacked. In the two years he had been with the group, there had been no criticism of any kind concerning his ability as a drummer.

The allegation that he wasn't a good enough drummer was completely without foundation, yet over the years it has grown to the extent that writers who were never there blithely repeat it. So not only was his future whipped away when he was on the brink of fame and fortune – but his reputation was maligned for decades to come.

I always considered this unfair, and was furious each time I came across pieces by writers who had never seen Pete perform with the Beatles, yet brought up the stale allegation that he was a poor drummer. When he was with the Beatles they were at their best as a live band. It was John Lennon himself who said, 'Our best work was never recorded, you know. We were performing in Liverpool, Hamburg and around the dance halls, and what we generated was fantastic.' It was also John who had the grace to say that the sacking of Pete Best was one of the most shameful episodes in the Beatles' career.

THE BEATLES

FIRST RECORD ON PARLOPHONE

LOVE ME DO

c/w

P.S. I LOVE YOU

RELEASED **FRIDAY OCTOBER 5th**

NEMS 12-14, WHITECHAPEL. Tel. ROYal. 7895
50, GREAT CHARLOTTE ST. 70-72, WALTON RD.

Epstein advertising the Beatles' first record in *Mersey Beat*. Pete actually recorded a version of 'Love Me Do' with the Beatles on Wednesday, 6 June 1962. The session was recorded by Ron Richards at EMI Studios, along with the numbers 'Besame Mucho', 'PS I Love You' and 'Ask Me Why'.

Over the years I was determined to make some sense out of that illogical move in 1962, which removed one of the main assets of the Beatles. According to various writers penning accounts of Beatles history, George Martin considered Pete's drumming to be so poor that he engaged Andy White to sit in for him. So I decided to trace at least some facts which could be corroborated.

The Beatles had been rejected by every major record label in Britain. Every pop label at EMI had turned them down without bothering to even audition them. It was only a freak stroke of luck that led the desperate Brian Epstein to the offices of George Martin.

Decca, whose representative had at least travelled to Liverpool to watch the group perform, and who had agreed to a recording audition, also gave Brian copies of their audition tapes. Purely by chance he noticed a tape-to-disc transfer service in the windows of the HMV record shop in Oxford Street, and took the tapes in. Some interest was shown in their original material and Sid Coleman of EMI's music publishing arm, Ardmore & Beechwood, which had an office in the HMV store, arranged for Brian to see Martin through his secretary.

Parlophone was not one of EMI's pop labels, but concentrated mainly on variety and comedy recordings. Martin had had success with artists such as Peter Sellers, an album of the 'Beyond the Fringe' revue and records by artists ranging from Bernard Cribbins to Jimmy Shand. Pop wasn't his field — he'd had the opportunity of signing Tommy Steele, but turned him down. (Steele then became the biggest British pop artist of the late 1950s.)

Martin had nothing to lose by signing the group, and offered them a paltry deal: a penny a single.

In Brian Epstein's biography, written by Ray Coleman, Brian's personal assistant Alistair Taylor said that Brian had blackmailed EMI into giving the Beatles the Parlophone deal: 'Brian threatened to withdraw his business from EMI if they didn't give them a recording contract . . . EMI took them on sufferance because Brian was one of their top customers. I saw Brian in tears, literally, because Martin promised to phone back and day after day went by and George Martin was never available, always "in a meeting".'

When the Beatles arrived at Abbey Road for their first recording session on Wednesday, 6 June 1962, it was Ron Richards who recorded them. When they began playing original material Richards went to see

Martin, who was in the canteen, and asked him to come and listen.

After the session, the only topic of discussion between Martin and Richards was whether to make one of them the group's leader, in the fashion of the time: John Lennon and the Beatles, or Paul McCartney and the Beatles. Martin finally decided to leave the group as they were.

Before the next EMI session, Pete was sacked. Why?

When Epstein used the excuse that George Martin had said that Pete wasn't a good enough drummer, Mona Best, as we know, phoned Martin. He told her, 'I never suggested that Pete Best must go. All I said was that for the purposes of the Beatles' first record I would rather use a session

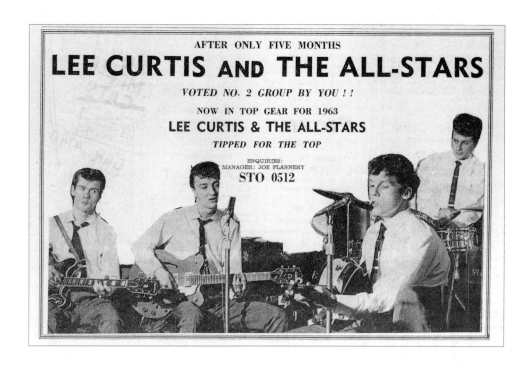

As this advertisement confirms, Lee Curtis & the All-Stars, who only formed a few months earlier, were voted into the No. 2 position immediately below the Beatles in the *Mersey Beat* poll, purely due to the fact that their new drummer was Pete Best.

man. I never thought that Brian Epstein would let him go. He seemed to be the most saleable commodity as far as looks went. It was a surprise when I learned that they had dropped Pete. The drums were important to me for a record, but they didn't matter much otherwise.'

A&R men in those days often used session drummers as a matter of course, mainly because of the particular recording sound they needed in a studio. They didn't have such technical problems with guitars and vocals. Andy White, for instance, was only one of several session drummers that George Martin and Ron Richards used frequently and felt happier working with.

After Pete was sacked, the Beatles, with their new drummer Ringo Starr, arrived at Abbey Road studios on Tuesday, 4 September, and recorded 'How Do You Do It' and 'Love Me Do'. Engineer Norman Smith was to comment, 'I've a feeling that Paul wasn't too happy with Ringo's drumming, and felt it could be better. He didn't make too good a job of it.'

They next went into the studio on Tuesday, 11 September, with Ron Richards as sole producer. He felt that the session with Ringo hadn't been good enough to produce a saleable first single, and Martin had apparently agreed with him.

Richards was to comment, 'We weren't happy with the drum sound on the original "Love Me Do", so I booked Andy White for the remake. I used him a lot of the time.'

So it seems that for all these years, the writers who were saying that George Martin had to book session musician Andy White because Pete Best wasn't good enough were wrong. Andy White was booked because the producer and engineer at the time didn't consider Ringo good enough.

Undisputed proof of Pete Best's amazing popularity in Liverpool. When Brian Epstein sent Bill Harry a cable informing him that the Beatles had signed with Parlophone, the front cover announcing the news featured a picture of Pete. It was also perhaps significant that the order of names in the announcement next to it was: 'Congratulations to Pete, Paul, John and George'.

Unfortunately, over the years people begin to believe the myths — even the ones in which they played a part. While Martin originally felt Pete was one of the group's assets, and didn't really worry about the drumming because he regularly used session drummers anyway, his memory over the years seems to echo the myths.

Pete leads his own band and Mike Smith at Decca – the same A&R man who'd originally turned down the Beatles when Pete was a member – signs them up. The group recorded 'I'm Gonna Knock on Your Door', released in June 1964, but it failed to chart and Decca lost interest.

I was also struck by the realisation that Pete Best probably spent more time performing live before audiences as a Beatle than Ringo did.

During that hectic two-year period as the band's drummer, Pete performed an incredible amount of actual stage time. In Hamburg alone he played hundreds of hours with the group. Back in Liverpool, when they were doing hour-long performances, sometimes two or three gigs a night, and over 200 performances at the Cavern alone, Pete also notched up considerable playing time.

Within months of Ringo joining, the group began their touring period, performing relatively short spots with set repertoires. They managed slightly more than 200 concert appearances, often with two performances at the concert venues, playing approximately eleven numbers a show.

If someone were to actually work out the total number of hours each drummer in the Beatles performed on stage before a live audience, I believe that Pete would emerge ahead.

19 ▶ COMRADES

Two years of working and playing long hours together unified the early Beatles. And the crucible of this transformation – the Liverpool and Hamburg of those wild times – gave their comradeship a unique vitality and creativity. Here Pete recalls the lads as he knew them, at the start of a momentous decade.

The camaraderie between us during those two years was something I'll always remember.

There was a lot of inspiration from Stu. Not musical creativity. When he played, what shone out was his effort and his belief in the band. I think if we'd said, 'Walk on water', he'd have done it, he believed in the band that much. He would talk to people and say, 'You know, they are going to make it, whether I'll be with them or not.'

Even after he'd left the band, he'd ask, 'What is happening with the band? How are they doing?' He was excited that we were coming back to Hamburg, and that he would see us again.

It was through the Casbah that I got to meet Stu before he and I ever became Beatles. When the Quarry Men played the club, he used to come along and watch because he was a friend of John's. Sometimes he would come and keep Cynthia company. This was before he even started to play bass guitar.

In those early days, John would tell me that Stu was a brilliant artist. As fate would have it, the next time I saw him was at my audition to become a Beatle – when I found that he was playing bass guitar with them.

Stu was the smallest member of the band, but like each individual, he had his own stage presence. He was often referred to then and later as having an image similar to James Dean's. Yet he was a happy-go-lucky fellow who never seemed to lose his

Left: George, John, Pete and Paul play together, a group who certainly seemed in harmony during 1960 to 1962. As a team they forged a sound and created a musical revolution. (Apple Corps)

temper. I've always said that what Stu lacked in technique he made up for in heart and effort.

It was while we were on our first Hamburg trip that I began to witness Stu's talent as an artist. He'd often sit down and sketch people from the audience.

His tragic death of a brain haemorrhage came in April 1962, while I was still a member of the Beatles.

The first time I saw John Lennon was when he came down with Paul McCartney, at the request of Ken Brown and George Harrison, to discuss the possibility of a Casbah residency. After the discussion with Mo they decided to reform the Quarry Men.

John had that art college look about him: white skintight pants or khaki denims (KDs for short) and a black lumberjack type jacket and black shirt. His hair was swept back in a quiff and he had sideburns to match – like Elvis Presley, the rocker look of those days.

He helped decorate part of the Casbah, particularly the ceiling in one of the smaller rooms. Because of his short-sightedness he painted it in black gloss rather than emulsion – that alone cost us a few bob to rectify!

One of the first things that struck me about him was his sense of humour and the crazy things he'd say or do. He didn't care a damn about what other people thought of him and he could be a hard man, with an abrasive wit and a very bad temper.

But there were two sides to him. The other was the very tender and loving person that the public never saw. I was fortunate to discover this when John and I would drink away the hours in Hamburg and Liverpool, and when he would come back after the gigs and sleep over in Hayman's Green.

It was as if his public image was a barrier for him to hide behind, preventing people from discovering the real John Lennon.

I was introduced to Paul at the same time as I first met John. My initial impression of him was that he was a very jovial, confident young person who would always like to be or try to be the centre of attention both on and off stage. John and Paul competed with one another in the humour stakes. There was a certain amount of one-upmanship going on between them and this element remained during the Hamburg and Liverpool days while I was still a member of the band.

Again, like a lot of people in those days, his hair was swept back, but his image wasn't as strong as John's.

Stuart. A tragic figure in the Beatles story, although he had left the group behind him at the time of his death. His artistic work is now highly collectable and his reputation has grown over the years, particularly since the release of the film biopic *Backbeat*.
(Astrid Kirchherr/Redferns)

Watching him in the Casbah and later playing with him in the group, I could see very early on that he had a wealth of talent and musical ability and a great vocal range.

In a way, I suppose Paul was the public relations person for the group, and was always the one to let everyone know what was happening to the band both at home and while we were in Germany. The fact that he and John became the songwriting team that the world knows today comes as no surprise to me. Even in those early days their talents shone through both individually and as a partnership.

George was the first member of the group I'd met. He used to play at a little venue in Hayman's Green called Lowlands, which was at the bottom end of the road. There was a skiffle and rock night each Sunday which was well attended by the locals – myself and my

John. Perhaps the Beatle who had the closest relationship with Pete. They spent many hours in each other's company, drinking, swapping yarns, forming a close comradeship. Their opinions about the Beatles' image also seemed to match. In a *Playboy* interview in 1980, when asked about why they fired Pete, John replied, 'The other lads wanted him out, but I think we made a mistake there. I mean, there were riots after Pete was sacked.'
(Astrid Kirchherr/Redferns)

Paul. The one Pete thought was the group's ideal PR man, dedicated to the group's success. (Astrid Kirchherr/Redferns)

mates included. At the time, George was playing guitar and singing in the Les Stewart Quartet, along with Ken Brown.

George was the youngest of us all and was often referred to as the baby of the group. He also wore his hair swept back in those days, and tight pants – the order of the day for any aspiring musician.

Once I got to know him, I realised that he was quite a shy person both on and off stage, but he was very much into his guitar playing and in striving to better himself. The long hours in Hamburg meant that this happened.

When we were together as a unit, George probably contributed as much as everyone else. At business meetings or at Brian's meetings he might listen, he might have something to say, but at that stage, he would usually roll with what was accepted overall.

There was banter among ourselves because he was the youngest in the band, but I know that as regards myself, I never excluded him from anything. He had the opportunity to express himself at all times and was free to choose the numbers he would play onstage, and free, like everyone else, to comment on what he felt about the group.

George would always join in any crazy antics which were taking place, but he was never an initiator in this sense, tending to follow rather than lead. George was a trendsetter in his own sweet way – being the first to get a leather jacket, first to get cowboy boots and the first to be sent home from Hamburg!

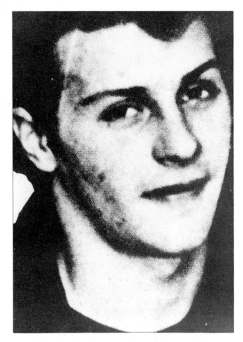

Pete.

When rumours of a talented newcomer swept the art college, I made it my business to get to know him. His name was Stuart Sutcliffe and we were kindred spirits. We got together to discuss so many things, art, literature, life in Liverpool, the future. I found him intense and dedicated to his art and envied his passion. No one, even in those early years, doubted his talent as an artist.

We got together with John and discussed our hopes for the future and how we would make Liverpool famous.

We were together on the Student's Union committee, ordering a PA system which the band could use at college dances. When I ran the film society, booking mainly Continental movies, Stu became fascinated by the Polish actor Zbigniew Cybulski, and began to wear tinted glasses like him. People mistakenly say he tried to look like James Dean when, in fact, Cybulski was his inspiration.

I thought it was a mistake when Stu joined the Beatles – and told him so. I felt that his talent as an artist would be compromised. But Stu loved the Beatles so much, and was so happy with them, that it was impossible not to accept the fact that he might have been sacrificing his talent as an artist to become a musician.

I was amazed by his transformation when I next saw him. He brought his fiancée, Astrid, to Liverpool with him and I remember the two of them at the Jacaranda, both pale, both dressed in black. Stu had an ashen pallor.

After his death I kept in touch with his mother, Millie, and we continued to talk about Stuart by phone every month until her own death. I remember her delight when I brought John around to see her – and she invited us to take our pick of Stu's work. John chose an oil painting, I picked an abstract collage.

John was striding round the college canteen when I first noticed him soon after he enrolled in 1957. His attitude and dress marked him out as a rebel. We became firm friends, teaming up with Stu and another student,

Rod Murray, for regular drinking sessions at Ye Cracke, and parties at students' flats. I became a visitor to Gambier Terrace when Rod, Stu and John shared a flat together. One night, up late talking, John suggested Virginia and I stay overnight and put us up in the bath! I wonder if he remembered that when he wrote 'Norwegian Wood'?

I was particularly impressed by John's ability as a writer and when we were alone, he'd show me his poetry. It was unique and hilarious, and his influences included Lewis Carroll, the Goons and Stanley Unwin. But it wasn't only his poetry and prose which intrigued me, it was also his artwork. John had a facility for creating humorous line drawings.

In 1960, when I decided to create Mersey Beat, I was determined to promote John's group, who we were booking regularly at the college dances. Before the Beatles left for Hamburg I told John about my plans for *Mersey Beat*, requesting that he write me a story about the group.

When I printed it without altering a single word, he was so delighted that he gave me all 250 of his poems and drawings, which I began to use in a regular column I called 'Beatcomber'.

John's Aunt Mimi said she always remembered me because I was the first person to call John a genius. Even in those days he had a powerful charisma and the Beatles became a fantastic live band.

I first met Paul on the steps of the art college. He and George were next door at Liverpool Institute and used to drop into our canteen and rehearse in the college life rooms with John and Stu. When I began *Mersey Beat*, it was Paul who always provided me with the information, sending me news of their recordings with Polydor, bringing me the Astrid Kirchherr and Jurgen Vollmer photos to print — and even photos by the talented Francis Michael (who turned out to be Paul's brother Mike).

Paul also used to write to me, and I considered his letters to be as funny and witty as John's in their own way. I found he had a genuine talent with words and a sense of humour which I don't think has really been appreciated over the years. He wrote to me from Hamburg, describing it as 'like Blackpool, but with strip clubs instead of lights!'

Paul could rock and roll with the best of them, particularly on the Little Richard numbers, but I always felt he was at his best on numbers which evoked feelings of romance, wistfulness, hope, melancholy and joy. His love songs were, I believe, among the best ever composed: 'And I Love Her', 'Here, There and Everywhere' are undoubted classics.

I believe it was Paul more than anyone else who became the driving force of the group. It might have begun as John's group, but with the emergence of Epstein as their manager, it transformed itself into Paul's group. He, more than any of the others, became dedicated to the success of the band and I believe the Beatles would have had a shorter career but for Paul's urging them to try new things.

Although George's position in the group was initially something akin to a younger sibling's, the first mention in print of an original Beatles composition was the story about 'Cry For a Shadow' in *Mersey Beat* which he had written. On the basis of this composition, I urged George to make an effort with his songwriting. I didn't know then that John and Paul were vying to get their own songs on the recordings, making it difficult for George to be heard. He had to take a back seat — but he was delighted when his breakthrough came with 'Don't Bother Me'. Yet it took Allen Klein to give George his first Beatles 'A' side, 'Something', which Frank Sinatra described as 'the greatest love song of the twentieth century'.

Ringo's company was most enjoyable. I used to drop round to see Ringo's mum, a most friendly hostess, always ready to put the kettle on for a cup of tea and a chat, and immensely proud of her son's success.

Ringo had an engaging humour and warm personality — and he proved his worth as an actor by getting the lion's share of attention in *A Hard Day's Night*.

He felt insecure at the beginning, when he joined the group, but soon became confident, especially in America where, for a time, he became the most popular Beatle, with over fifty novelty discs dedicated to him.

I used to sit and talk with Pete Best at the Blue Angel. I realise now that when it came to interviews he was a laconic character — a man of few words, to coin a phrase — but he also had undoubted charisma and the girls went crazy over him.

When he was sacked there was local fury, and cries of 'Pete forever, Ringo never' at the Cavern. George was given a black eye and Brian Epstein had to have bodyguards because of the fans' intense rage at the time.

Since that time, Pete — who's never held a grudge about the sacking — attempted to forge a career in music with his Pete Best Four, without success. So he went elsewhere to earn a livelihood. His sacking still remains a mystery. But through it all, Pete has persevered, and he now has a beautiful wife and two daughters, a strong family presence in the West Derby area and lots of very loyal friends.

Perhaps, after all these years, his time has come.

Pete today, performing on a world tour with The Pete Best Band, originally formed in 1989. On the band's first CD, *Live At The Adelphi*, Pete's powerful drumming is complemented by his younger brother Roag, who doubles on drums. The two-drummer line-up is unique in a band focusing on music from the 1960s and 1970s. Their second CD, *Back to the Beat*, was recorded live at the Cavern in August 1994 and their most recent release was *Once A Beatle: Always* in October 1996.

EPILOGUE

Tommy Moore, whose stint as the Silver Beatles' drummer lasted less than two months, was later to join a local jazz band. He died of a stroke in 1981.

Mona Best, the pioneering promoter, died on 9 September 1988 following a heart attack.

Allan Williams and his wife Beryl have parted company. Allan is still a popular guest at Beatles conventions.

Lord Woodbine's real name remains a mystery.

Bettina Derling, the *bier frau* who was so much in love with John Lennon, ended up managing one of the houses in the Herbertstrasse, the street of windows. Julian Lennon visited her to ask for memories of his father. She became very ill in 1996.

George Martin retired in 1996, during which year he was awarded a knighthood in the Queen's Birthday Honours.

Brian Epstein was found dead on 27 August 1967. His death was said to be accidental, caused by an overdose of tablets. He was thirty-two years old.

Horst Fascher still lives in Hamburg, having unsuccessfully attempted to revive the Star Club name by opening rock venues in the city.

Tony Sheridan teamed up with Howie Casey and Roy Young late in 1995 to revive the Beat Brothers.

By 1996 Derry Wilkie (of Derry and the Seniors) had settled in London's Hampstead area, and Freddie Starr had established himself as one of Britain's leading comedians.

Rosa, the little old lady the Beatles called 'Mutti', died in the early 1990s.